The Almighty's Religion for the Universe

The Almighty's Religion for the Universe

Rev. Sidney R. Smith, MHS

Copyright © 2018 Rev. Sidney R. Smith, MHS
All rights reserved
First Edition

URLink Print and Media
Cheyenne, Wyoming

First originally published by URLink Print and Media. 2018

ISBN 978-1-64367-015-7 (Paperback)
ISBN 978-1-64367-014-0 (Digital)

Printed in the United States of America

Foreword

Santorino-
A High Spirit of God

My 29, 1944

"Do not call on the people to desecrate and destroy their gods. Rather, respectfully place them in the hall of the Almighty as diversified images of the one and same God, created by nations with different understandings and perceptions. -- Christ, Buddha, Mohammed, Zoroaster, Confucius, and the gods of other nations will stand in the temple of God next to each other and will remind humankind of its spiritual essence and the various depictions of God in the hearts of different nations".

"The new faith [Supplementology] is coming not to destroy the old gods, but to unify them in a single, true God who will rule all the nations . . . with justice, love and omniscience..."

The Nine Norms

1. God will not perform miracles or save the world from the clutches of evil. The Almighty has given mankind free will: the choice between doing good and evil.
2. Prayer to God proves meaningless. Only doing good deeds and action matter. Actions and good deeds are the true prayers producing results.
3. Humanity has deviated from the teachings of Christ so greatly that little remain of them. Heinous crimes have been committed in the name of religion. Hence the need for SUPPLEMENTOLOGY: unifying all mankind and shedding new light on universal faith.
4. Children are the future of humanity. Parent's main focus shall be raising children properly, tirelessly, and persistently from a child's first day of his life until adulthood. In addition to comprehensive education, the most important subject to be taught in schools is establishing a successful family life and properly raising children.
5. God and The Almighty do not reward, punish, or destroy. Mankind alone shall resolve to overcome the needs of matter (accumulation of material and

physical wealth) and recognize spiritual reward, responsibility, and accountability.

6. Paradise and Hell are here and now, they exist only as mankind has created them on Earth and in the minds of mankind. They have no place in The Almighty's created world. Hell is eternal nonexistence (loss of spiritual individuality) for all spirits that do not comply with the will and law of God and Heaven is eternal spiritual existence in the entire universe.

7. Man consists of both spirit and matter. Components of matter, such as the brain help the spirit reach a higher level of divinity and spiritual individuality helping to overcome the needs of flesh (matter) and material gain.

8. Every living human being possesses an immortal spirit. Every human being must come to understand that in actuality there is truly no such thing as death.

9. God's and Satan's spirit were created from the spirit of The Almighty. God cannot rule over Satan nor can Satan rule over God. God and Satan have their own particular duties and functions. The function of Satan and His spirits are to: bolster living things; form the strength of the body and the spirit; mold the inferior; test the weak; give human beings an understanding of logic and law. The function of God and His spirit are to: protect living beings from perishing; bring the idea of love and mercy to human beings; overcome doubt and inspire faith in goodness and in eternity.

Let Me Not Be Passive

Let me not be passive, while someone leads me into a steel
door and breaks my nose.
Let me not be passive,
while someone steps on my feet and breaks my toes.
Let me not be passive,
for another 700 years while life's chances
Pass me by.
Let me not be passive, but assertive, aggressive if I must
for the days of passivity have diminished my trust,
while others reap false claim to my hard work
and bask in glory of my servitude.
Oh, No! No More!
If I must be passive, I'll choose the time and place,
as long as it's done in dignity and not in disgrace.
I will not linger long in stagnant ineptitude,
while fakes reach for heights that have no depth.
The embellishment of fate sends me to heights
that visions have yet to unfold
and I wait passively for the enrichment of my soul.

By Venita Bernee Colbert & Sidney Smith, May 2, 1998
Composed during a discussion on the fate of humanity.

Preface

Dear readers it has been six years since I published my first book dealing with the subject matter that this new publication will also express. I have not changed the contents, I am just revisiting and summarizing this preface. As I am conscious of the fact that The Almighty, God, and the chief spirits of the universe are observing my actions and deeds, it is now a matter for humanity to recognize that it is being observed as well. This is the first and last time that this information will be revealed to humanity. We can listen to these Messages and begin to reunite the human race, or we can allow these Messages to dissipate into non-existence.

My first book "Search for the Promised Land/How to Bring Religion and Science into Harmony" did not convey the Messages as I would have liked. I along with Nick Mezins and Maya Homics have had to undergo a transformation. Since we realize that The Almighty in most peoples minds is another way to describe God, we had to decide on how we could effectively explain The Almighty as a single entity separate from God. Since Jesus was not able to explain to His Apostles whom the Holy Ghost was in biblical times. Humanity is now allowed to realize that the Holy Ghost, whom Jesus Christ spoke of was not God His Father, but a separate entity that is invisible, incomprehensible and unapproachable by any spirit including God. You will learn that even the chief spirits of the universe exclaim, "They are like dust beneath His feet".

I contacted several marketing firms with a request for a proposal to help us develop a name for our religion. Buzzmaiketing.com presented several options and Mr. Mark Hughes/President, accepted the challenge. We, never however, fully came together to explore the fullest potential of getting these Messages to the public.

Suppelmentology and its Nine Norms were created from the information that was revealed to the original Message Bearers in 1943 through 1971. These revelations have been in existence for the past 63 years and known as

"The Almighty's Religion for the Universe". Since most people cannot differentiate The Almighty from God, we choose to call it S upplementology. It still is however, essentially the same as it has been for these past 63 years. The name represents what also this religion intends to do. That is to supplement all religions with new information so that all religions will be understood as one and the same teachings from God to mankind.

Let me retrospect briefly at this point to the present time. It has been a 27 years struggle to reveal these new religious revelations to humankind. I now can imagine that all of the envoys of God to this planet had to go through the same ordeal I have encountered. This is not to say I am a prophet or envoy of God. Please do not misinterpret. I am just saying that to reveal new revelations from God requires determination and perseverance on the part of the individual and a belief that the task must be done under all circumstances and challenges. Despite, the opposition of those who wish to believe in the contemporary and traditional perspective of their religious faith, one must have courage, strength, and wisdom to overcome the obstacles and barriers which one must face.

Let me give a partial list of those with whom I tried to convey this information to:

1. Rev. Dirk Ficca, Executive, Director, Council for a Parliament of World Religions
2. Mr. Richard Ostling, Religious Editor, Associated Press
3. Ms. Amy Edelstein, Editor, Enlightenment Magazine
4. Ms. Joy Kinnon, Senior Editor, Ebony Magazine
5. Mr. Julia Duin, Religious Editor, The Washington Times Newspaper
6. Dr. Phillip Hefner, Director, Chicago Center for Religion and Science
7. Ms. Adelle M. Banks, Senior Correspondent, Religious News Service
8. Mr. Bill Broadway, Religious Editor, Washington Post Newspaper
9. Ms. Diane Connolly, Religious Links Editor, Religious News Writers Association.

I am not faulting these people for not providing this information to the public I only hope you the reader understand the hurdles I have encountered with little or no result. In the attempt to present new religious revelations to humanity the press members and others have violated our rights to be heard. These people that received these Messages and transmitted them to humanity as well as myself have a right to be heard.

The God we speak of is the same God that mankind has worshipped since the beginning of religious doctrine. Our religion, however, will "SUPPLEMENT" and "SUPERSEDE" all religions of the world. This religious revelation is radically different from all religious beliefs, therefore the press and our religious institutions can be critical, skeptical, and judgmental about what is being revealed.

America was established on the basis of the Constitution. The First Amendment guarantees the freedom of expression; the freedom to believe in God as we choose; the freedom to be heard. Press members and religious institutions not only denied and impeded this information. None of them even took the time to investigate these revelations. They simply did not attempt to authenticate or verify its noteworthiness or validity.

I am not a scholar, theologian, nor emissary of God. I know, however, that these people that came from Latvia, by way of Germany after WWII, arrived in America with a vision and a mission. I am sure they came to America for the specific reason of our constitution. It is because we as American citizens are allowed to express different points of view that we do not fear persecution or ostracism.

The duty and responsibility of the press is to share information and let others become the judge of an expressed faith or belief. Our treasured freedom of the American Constitution cannot be violated because of the press or individual criticism, skepticism, or opinion. The "Message Bearers"

left Latvia and Germany because of their commitment, sacrifice, and belief in a "new religious revelation" which were given to them by God, and The Almighty to save our world.

Many of you may feel the same as the press and current religious leaders, that a new religion is not needed since mankind has believed in the teaching of the prophets for many centuries. Each religion institution has taken the position that God is on its side. Yet, we see our world in turmoil and confusion. Each religious institution is composed of different nations and races. Now the time has come to see that all spirits are created from the same source making all humans equal as spiritual beings existing in bodies (matter). Now we must recognize the true meaning of reincarnation and immortality as spirits and human beings. This information puts forth the understanding that we as human beings are composed of two distinct substances, matter and spirit. For the first time in human history, new information from God and His spirits confirms the knowledge about our spirituality. As difficult as it may seem, we must realize how the ancient truths did not fully answer the question of mankind's origin. What mankind was able to comprehend 6,000 years ago must be compared to what your parents were able to explain to you as a child. Your parents used fairy tales and fables to explain the meaning of life. A child is told that a new born baby is delivered by the stork, what sense would it make to you if you had been given the real truth about reproduction at the age of two? God was unable to give the real truth to mankind about creation 6,000 years ago, but now mankind has grown up. We want real answers to the questions of the ages. So now we are being given the true answers to creation, life, and the universe.

    Science and technology have advanced mankind to the point of not allowing us to identify with the Bible and other books of religion. We want real answers that correlate with the discoveries of science. Even though science does not have all the answers humanity still wants to relate its discoveries to God. Whatever mankind uncovers has, however, everything to do with God. Discoveries and inventions will never cease because we will never know as much as God. God has been in existence for billions of years and mankind is still in the process of developing through His knowledge and creation of humanity, other living beings, (plants and animals) as well as, our galaxy, and our planet.

    I have come to realize that I am a part of the human race not the race I am identified as being. There is no one better than me and I am no better than anyone else. My function is to try and love my fellow human beings. That is why I have taken the time to get this information to the public. It is because I only wish to show my love and respect for God and humanity. I want peace on this Earth, I want to see poverty end, and I want to come back to a world of paradise and harmony. I am alone in this faith and there is no other way for me to make possible my desires except through this new religious faith.

I will end my revision at this point. Yet, I must say one more thing to those that wish to enter this new realm. Unlike any other religious event that has happened before you will feel and sense new spirits talking to you and observing your thoughts. For centuries we have only felt and known of the existence of God, hence, we have become comfortable with His intervention in our lives. We pray to God in our time of need and discomfort and He answers us with truth and knowledge. This time however other spirits of The Almighty have given us new and different answers to the questions that have so long prevailed in the minds of mankind.

We are no longer children of God but adults, able to comprehend the true meaning of our existence and His desires for humanity. Just as all new revelations from God these revelations too will be met with consternation and contempt. Despite it all I feel they will help mankind overcome the confusion about what is real and what is imagined. Our world must develop as a result of the plans that God has put forth. We must be willing to try and understand the will of God even if it means accepting a new religious faith. Revelations from God provides a new truth so that we can transform our world for the benefit of all humanity.

Throughout the age of mankinds existence there has been various forms of religious convictions, conventions, and traditions. From primitive men to modem man, human being have sought to understand the basic elements of life, as well as the natural and unnatural laws of life. This has led mankind to worship the physical elements that affects our planet. From the sun god to the gods of earth, air, and sea, mankind has paid particular attention to the harnessed powers of his world. Today, we do not worship the same things that our primitive ancestors worshipped; yet we still worship an unseen power, this power known to many as God, the creator of our world and as such, we pay homage to His unseen presence. But is religion simply the praying and worshipping of God?

For centuries mankind has looked to God for their salvation and continued comprehension of this world and the universe. In many cases, mankind has found relief in the words that God has sent to this planet by His envoys or messengers. Yet, we find, for the most part, we have become lost in a sea of religious beliefs and understanding. Mankind is still trying to determine which religious faith is correct. There are so many different religious philosophies that sometimes one can become confused as to whether or not a God does actually exist.

We know that Jesus Christ, Mohammed, Buddha, and Confucius proclaimed the existence of some laws and rules that control the nature of mankind's behavior. These rules came about from a need to make mankind aware of his moral obligation toward other men. Yet, to this day, some people still doubt the origin of these laws, all the messengers taught the same basic laws of loving one another and believing in eternity.

Human beings have, for the most part, come to rely on the messages that were provided to them. Christians believe, however, only their laws are binding and connected to the will of God. The same can be said of those that believe and are followers of other religious faiths. Mankind has inherited a condition of turmoil and confusion surrounding the question of religious faiths. Each religion has been broken down into a wide array of denominations or sects, each denomination and sect requiring that one-follow different doctrines regarding the faith which it espouses.

Today, many followers of religion look to their religious leaders to provide them with answers concerning their own particular faith. The answers they receive are based on their religious leader's interpretation of the messages, which had been provided by an envoy, sent to our planet and their nation. These messages, which can be considered ancient as they relate to when they were received, are still considered viable for today's world. Still, the same question remains: what is religion? How does religion affect the lives of human beings in our current time? Is there a need to continue believing in something that cannot be proven to exist? Since we no longer believe in the same gods as our primitive ancestors, is it appropriate to reason that God does not exist either?

To answers to these questions and more, the Message Bearers revealed from these religious revelations a new truth. First I propose that we take a look at the question of religion. What is it?

Religion is a force that controls the nature of all creation. It is the will of the Creator that incorporates and generates the laws of physics throughout the universe. In that sense, we must come to terms with The Almighty's religion - this religion encompasses all of the religions of this world and the entire universe. Religion is not only the capability to worship and pray to God, it is the following of The Will of the Almighty to help create the ideal world.

One must come to understand that the Creator was at one time alone in this universe, and this means that He had to be His own pupil and teacher. He did not have sample from which to create life. Before there was a universe consisting of planets, stars, and other heavenly bodies, there was only The Almighty, matter, and energy. Since matter and energy had no purpose or goal, The Almighty had to investigate and research this lifeless world of matter and energy. He created from this purposeless world of matter and energy a purpose. The Almighty created religion as a means for His creations to follow certain laws, which would provide for the continued existence of orderly and organized matter and energy. Therefore, the law of gravity is ruled by religion. All the forces of nature are ruled by religion. The animal and plant life of our planet are ruled by religion. It must be seen that religion is the guiding force for everything in the universe. All living things, as well as non-living things, are ruled by religion. No longer must we commit ourselves to determining which religion is correct, but rather we must begin to assess and evaluate our understanding of religion in a new and provocative way.

Before our planet and other solar systems were created there was the existence of religion. Religion did not come about as a result of the messages that were delivered by the envoys of God. These messages were given to a people that could not understand the very essence of religion. They had not obtained enough knowledge to understand the basis law of physics. Jesus the greatest genius of life could not convey to His wisest disciple the law of gravity, nor the simple chemical makeup of water (which I am sure many people of today are aware is H20). How then can we make a comparison to religions of our past and relate them to our current time?

The religions of today are the product of past generations. This is not to say that these religions of the past and the present are not important and therefore should be disregarded. On the contrary, they stand as a testament to God's will toward mankind, His will to love and protect us from all harm. In His will to love and care for us, He has sent envoys with messages to instruct us about religion. Now, however, mankind does not need any special person to convey the laws of religion. Mankind now has the power to teach himself about the rules and laws of religion in a new way, and this means coming to terms with a new definition of religion. Religion is distinctively one element, encompassing the existence of all living and non-living things. There is nothing living or lifeless that is not affected by religion. The Almighty created all living things and His religious laws guide everything in the universe. This religious law, which rules the law of physics for the entire universe, is the new religion that is being revealed.

A new message has been heralded to mankind, and not in the familiar way as before. No envoy has been provided to deliver these messages about The Almighty's religion. God knows that we have reached a point where we can no longer live by the ancient rules of our ancestors. He has allowed mankind to receive these new religious revelations in a different way. This has happened because He trusts our ability to understand the importance of these new revelations.

Just as we have shown Him our capacity to change the existing laws of nature (to the extent that mankind does not suffer from the impacting laws of nature (we have air conditioning in the boiling heat of summer and the comfort of artificial heat for the frigid elements of winter), we have proved to God that we are capable of utilizing material elements to change our environment. Mankind does not need to ask God for protection from the environment. Mankind now asks God to provide the means for maintaining his basic needs. It is because of this request that God has revealed His new religious revelations to humanity.

As mankind enters the new millennium, these religious revelations and confirmations can propel humanity toward a new sense of accomplishment. These messages help to give new objectives and goals, which will be for this planet and the entire universe. Religion is the force, which helps mankind to reach a level of perfection through enlightenment; religion does not demand the perfection of mankind; rather, it provides for the further elevation of humanity to the heights of omni comprehension and omniscient. Comprehension of the universe and ourselves allows us to have faith in what we cannot see, yet understand.

Religion is having faith that the sun will use. Although we know the sun will rise, the question for our ancestors was, "How does it rise?" Mankind has reached a point where it has discovered the empirical laws and principles of the sun. We know gravity holds the sun in place, and we know the elements that keeps it burning and alive. We know that our planet revolves around the sun, yet we never question how these laws of physics were created. We can assume that God created these laws; however, our religious teaching never state in fact that He did. All we know as Christians is that He spontaneously created the earth in six days. Ask yourself: "Wouldn't it seem more plausible for people of ancient time to believe this explanation of creation?" Scientists have explored and researched the answer to creation and they explain it differently.

People for the first time must consider that the law of religion rules the way in which all elements of the universe operate. Before there was a gravitational force there was none; before there was a planet Earth there was none. In other words, nothing comes from nothing. There has to be something before there can be something. Someone has to exist before something can be made to exist. Imagine that our great composers, inventors, and scientists could create things with just their will. They would first have to create elements, which would guide the implements of their will. The will is intangible and invisible. A person may think, but is anyone able to use their will to bring into existence material objects? Impossible as it may seem, there is only one entity that has the power to complete this feat. And that is The Almighty. His will is religion. Before He created objects from matter and energy, He had to discover all of matter's peculiar and particular properties and how they relate to one another. Once He experimented with various hypotheses, He concluded that it should remain that way. The law of gravity is a religious law bound to the heavenly bodies by The Almighty. It was through the Creator's will that everything in the universe, including man, was created; therefore, these new religious revelations can help mankind achieve a better understanding and consolidation of all religious laws and principles on the planet Earth as we come to understand "Supplementology". (The Almighty's Religion for the Universe")

Introduction

In the course of my life's journey, I have constantly wondered about the truth of religion. There have been a great number of questions, which I pondered. I lived on the knowledge of what I was taught in Sunday school, and through my living within the framework of society's beliefs. I was perplexed and confused about my faith in God and Jesus' teachings. I was told in Sunday school to love and care about my fellow human being, but was this an absolute commandment of God? How could I love my fellow man when, in reality, my fellow man did not conform to those things, which I had been taught to believe?

This monumental path of indecision started in 1957 when I was only 7 years old. I had not yet experienced the knowledge of God or Satan. In fact, until this point I followed my basic instincts in relation to doing good or bad; my previous experience dealt mostly with conditioned behavior. If I misbehaved then I was rewarded with negative discipline, and for doing good, positive reinforcement. I did not, however, equate these elements with anything other than just doing something to stay out of trouble or to receive a special treat. Nevertheless, I did as most small children do: I did what I was told to do. Yet I was inquisitive and active.

The day came when I was thrust into the realm of religion. There on the wall of our new home was a depiction of something so horrible that I was frightened beyond description. I saw three posters depicting terrible human suffering. In the clutches of the giant beasts claws were people being tortured and devoured. This beast stood taller than any building I had ever seen. People were trampled under its feet, building demolished, and there was wreckage and chaos everywhere. I could not comprehend what this scene represented. I went to bed that night with those grotesque pictures staring down upon me. There was large neon sign that flashed throughout the night as I hid under my covers, the blinking light reminding me that those awful pictures were still there.

In the morning, with a great sense of relief that I had made it though the night, I asked my new guardian what those pictures meant. It was then that I was told of the concept of heaven and hell. Those pictures were the depiction of the last days for humanity. I was told that the pictures were the representation of the Book of Revelations in the Bible. The people in the beast's claw were sinners, and Satan with the forces of evil was claiming their victims. This was my initiation into religion: doing good resulted in receiving a reward of going to heaven and to do bad was the punishment of dreadful hell.

From that day on I did all I could to learn what the standards were for doing good. I learned various passages of the Bible, the Ten Commandments, and prayed to God to help me do good and forgive me for my sins. I was determined not to end up in the clutches of Satan and the inevitable hell of fire and brimstone, which was destined for all sinners. As I grew older, however, it became apparent to me that something was amiss. The world's inhabitants appeared to be moving toward their own course for destruction. I witnessed the era of world powers creating weapons of destruction. The A-bomb, ICBMs, and bomb shelters were the common topics being discussed. These things seemed more relevant than the coming of God on resurrection day. Rather than the world becoming a better place to live, it appeared that our world was becoming more horrible. As I grew older, my actions and deeds were geared toward doing good. In school, the community, and my church, I tried to exemplify that which I had learned. I had become so conditioned in the belief of love and respect for all God's creatures that I began to avoid stepping on ants instead of crushing them. I realized the beauty of life, no matter how small, was in all that lived and breathed. Consequently, I expected other children to join me in my efforts to do good and be obedient to God's law. Instead, the other children seemed to enjoy killing ants. They resorted to finding ant mounds and poking objects into the entrance, and in response to the defending ants' efforts to save their homes, the children (who were taught the same laws to love and value life as I) did not care they were taking lives aimlessly and needlessly. I tried to reinforce my belief in this faith by studying as much of the Bible as possible. I was able to quote passages from the Bible with earnestness and faith. Often in Sunday school I would answer questions that the other children didn't know.

I became so good at memorizing the Bible that I began to engage in conversations with adults about the Bible and its contents. Once during an outing with other churches at a picnic there was a contest to determine who knew the most about the Bible. Children and adults were invited to participate. A prize was to be given to the person who answered the most questions correctly. Well, I won! The adults became agitated over the fact that I could answer more than they. I didnt get my prize for several weeks, and that was only after I constantly reminded them of my winning the contest.

I began to discover that my faith and convictions concerning love, truth, and justice were often inconsistent with life's trials and tribulations for the human race. I asked myself: What is wrong with the human race? Had not man been promised an everlasting life in heaven or hell? "I believed in God and so I prayed for His divine intervention while I witnessed the savage desecration of His law to love one another in peace, harmony, and brotherhood.

Other laws were being violated as well . My childhood conscience was susceptible to believing any truth expressed to me. I was told to believe in the laws of God, as interpreted by any particular denomination. The denomination that initiated my religious faith taught me various laws that conformed to their beliefs. It was a sin to watch TV; it was a sin to believe or honor any holiday other than Thanksgiving; it was a sin to eat pork; it was a sin to attend a movie except to see something religious or biblical. How did these laws address humanity's needs? I asked myself. As I grew older, I realized that hunger, destitution, and poverty were more prevalent and needed to be attended to, more so than these "sins" which were committed based on man's technological advances. Many times I passed a movie theater or a store window filled with TVs and I smelled the fresh aroma of steamed sausages waft through the air from the outdoor vendor's cart, and wished that God would rescind His laws concerning these rules I had to observe. It was shameful for me to wish for those things that were forbidden; yet I also wished that those who were suffering the pangs of hunger and poverty would be relieved of their pain and sorrow. Why were they suffering and had they committed sins that were so terrible that there was no possible redemption?

Those laws didn't stop there: I was not allowed to associate with the children who lived next to our home. I often saw the other children playing and frolicking around in their yard. I became curious as to why I wasn't allowed to play with them. The song of "Jesus loves the little children, all the children of the world" was a tune I constantly recited in my mind because, for me He was always there. But why couldn't I play with these children? The simple explanation was that they were not saved and would end up in the abyss of hell. Mother, father, and children were consigned to hell and isolation because they did not follow the rules of our God.

Of course, I found ways to speak with these children. With careful planning and scheming, I discussed with them their particular dilemma. They were going to hell and I was going to heaven. I was soon to discover however that they did not believe in Jesus Christ or the gospel of the Bible. They were Jewish, they explained to me. I learned that they were not going to suffer as a result of not obeying the Bible; only because they lived by the rules of something they called the Torah. Somehow they were not given the same privileges as everyone else because of their nationality and their religious beliefs. They were isolated and ostracized because or their religious convictions. Their parents were not beggars, criminals, convicts, or robbers, yet at the same time, they were bound for hell simply because they were of a different faith than mine. It didn't make sense.

By the time I reached nine years of age, I had to move to another home. By now, I had been totally indoctrinated to the truth of religion; at least I thought so. The first morning of my life in this new environment I was subjected to the strength and conviction of my faith. Bacon and eggs were being prepared for breakfast. Having been taught that pork was unclean and a sin to consume, I refused to eat the bacon and the eggs because they had been fried in pork grease, I thought back to an incident in which I committed the most dreadful sin ever. I had been sent to the store to purchase a pound of vegetable shortening. The grocer was, however, out of the product of which I had been sent to purchase. He told me that I could substitute it with lard. Being young and inexperienced, I accepted the pound of lard. I then proceeded home and gave the contents of my purchase to my guardian. She immediately became agitated and distressed, and began to wail and moan over my having committed the worst sins. I was severely disciplined and prayed over for having committed such a horrible deed. The house was fumigated and exorcised because pork has passed the portals of our sanctum.

Having undergone such an extreme reaction, I did not ever want to see, taste or touch pork again, but what was I to do? In this new home, it was not a sin to eat pork, yet I had been taught otherwise. My refusal to eat pork only created more grief. There were invariably meals of smothered pork chops, baked ham, sandwich of bologna, potted meat and, of course breakfasts of bacon and sausage. Could I give up eating these things altogether?

Could I just wait for the grand coming of God and eventual kingdom of heaven? This dilemma ate at my conscience. At the same time I was trying to obey the law of God, I was also hungry. My stomach eventually overruled my conscience and belief, and so I willingly ate pork. But what were the consequences for doing this wrongful deed? Could I pray to God and ask Him to forgive me, and would I still be saved from going to hell? What could I do before my death to save my soul?

So now the question of death became most urgent in my mind. I was a child perplexed and frightened about death. My involvement with religious institutions taught me to fear hell and to do good in order to receive eternal life and go to heaven, for on the reckoning of my death, I would go to one place or the other for all eternity. Growing up only added to my confusion about death. The question of death became not only complex and perplexing, but paradoxical as well. "One day we will live and never die." "In the holy name of God we are and shall always be. "These phrases created an impression in my mind of standing before a granite mountain, impregnable, unmovable, and unchangeable. I had no way of understanding what immortality or eternity meant. What could I look forward to in terms of eternal life? Would I live this eternal life in body or spirit?

Consequently, I was propelled into young adulthood with unresolved issues surrounding religion. As an adult, I began to experience a doubt and dissatisfaction with religious truth and God. There was a conglomeration of religious doctrines of which I had to choose. There was not only the Christian faith, but also Islam, Buddhism, Judaism, as well as other faiths. I became confused and disoriented so much so that I reached a point where I didn't believe in God or His evil counterpart, Satan. My disenchantment led me on the path of atheism. So I set about to discover and reveal to the world my understanding of life and its meaning.

It was in 1972 that I discovered something that I thought was mind shattering. It was while I was attending college that I met a professor who was in the process of establishing a social institution based on the principle of what he termed "The Genius Transformation for Life Creed." This creed stated that "We (each and all of us) are Genius: The Creation and Carriers of great extraordinary Creative life power: Bom with the Power, the Means, and the Methods, the Authority, and Responsibility to transform the world of social institutions and artifacts, for life's abundant growth and reproduction, in creative freedom and peace, Here and Now." This statement became the purpose of my very existence. I now could resolve my issue to remain humane without the principles of God's teachings. As such, I participated in the development of a special project directed at providing humanity with a new way to develop social institutions dealing with this principle. After a while, however, I became discontented with this ideal as well.

I sought the solitude of my own thoughts. I became introverted and insolated from the world, seeking only the security of family life and benefits of such. I worked hard to establish the daily routine of adjusting to society's demands, and then I was tossed into a situation, which really made me become totally indifferent to God. My soul mate's life was cruelly and savagely ended when she was raped and murdered. Her disappearance remained shrouded in mystery for six weeks. I begged God to bring her safely back to me. I would sacrifice my own life if only He would just let me see her alive and well again. But that was not to be as her body wad finally recovered. That episode in my life changes my attitude toward life and all religious principles.

I had nothing but contempt for God and Satan. I didn't believe in heaven or hell. If I died then I would jut become dust and dirt. Life had no value or meaning. I stayed in a state of mourning for at least a year and a half. I was reckless and disrespectful of life and God. I didn't care if I lived or died; that is, until I came very close to death itself. I did not believe that death would be anything but final life. As such, I tried to challenge death and life. As a result, one summer day a friend of mine invited me to a cast party with some of her colleagues. She saw the affect that the death of my significant one was taking its toll on me. I was depressed and distressed

I had been told that the effects of the combination of alcohol and amphetamine would boost my sensation of being intoxicated, but I was not told that the combination of these two substances could be lethal if mixed. So I obtained some amphetamines (black beauties) of which I took three pills. I went to the play in which my friend was performing.

After the performance, we went to several nightclubs after which I had several drinks. By the time we decided to get something to eat at a restaurant, I began to feel a sensation that I had never experienced before. Describing this feeling is a bit difficult; however, I felt as if my life was waning away from me. I was later told that with the amount of drugs and alcohol I had in my system it could have caused my death. I knew this was true because when I went to the rest room I laid down on the floor, my heart was palpitating, my breath was short and shallow, and I felt as if my body was moving into a state of unconsciousness. I felt the presence of death ready to take me into the next realm of life. Upon reaching the gateway of death, I reconsidered this option to life. I wanted to live. I wasn't overcome with a vision or anything I just knew God existed, because He saved me from death. My profusion of prayers to God in my desperation to get a second chance to life was answered.

I now wanted to get back on my feet, so to speak. I went back to work and made every attempt to become reconciled with the duties of life and survival. I still believed in the principles of what I had learned on my own and in the teachings of God. I somehow wanted to combine the essence of both.

In the course of my redemption and reconciliation with God I decided to "save the world" as it were. I became an ordained minister, but I chose to deal with a new religious concept: I was not going to be a traditional or conventional religious leader. I promised to work with God to help deal with establishing a new social system that would only benefit humanity. And so in this vein I wrote a series of letters explaining my concerns and a possible solution to world problems. I developed a mailing list that was comprised of presidents, prime ministers, kings and queens of every nation on earth, all the members of the U.S. Congress and

Senate, every world religious leader, including the Pope and the delegation in the Vatican, every newspaper and magazine editor, and every owner of radio and T V stations. The total number of people on the list consisted of over three thousand people.

After I completed this monumental task, to my chagrin, I received only five consolatory letters and one letter of total disdain. Shortly after this bitter disappointment I was ready to pursue this avenue again. I was determined to give to the world an opportunity to discover what I considered a new path for humanity to travel. I wasn't after any reward or recognition for my efforts; I just wanted to express my newfound convictions. I considered my ideas important because I felt that God had given me this chance to redeem myself. He had provided me with a vehicle that would help me to achieve my lofty goal of making the world a better place to live.

In the course of composing my series of letters to world leaders, the gentleman who was editing my work donated some discarded books to the organization where I worked. The box contained several books dealing with other people's concepts and religious philosophies relating to different spectrums of life. In my quest to gain some additional insight and knowledge regarding other people opinions and thoughts, I began to read some of their material.

In this collection of books there was one entitled "Messages to Mankind from the Almighty and His Spirits" by Alexander Homics. Upon my initial encounter with this book, I was convinced that the contents were fictional.

Nothing, I had seen on the TV program "The Twilight Zone" had ever put me in a state of amazement as this book had done. At first it frightened me, but every time I read it, I found something totally and inexplicably different. It guided me in the direction of understanding the truth of creation, religion, God, Satan, and spirituality in a totally different way.

This book gave me a new perspective and concept in dealing with religion.

Where I had drawn abstract opinions and ideas about life, this book changed my views completely. What had I discovered? Was it really true, the knowledge it was conveying? Where could I go to gain some confidence, explanation, and verification of this new knowledge? No preacher would understand, no friend, no wife, no sibling, no parent, no loving relative, absolutely no one would even consider the possibility of what I discovered. I reviewed this information for four years and during this time I didn't have anyone with whom to collaborate. I decided to conform to the teaching of these messages, and for the past twenty-six years I have journeyed this new path. Now I would like for you to journey with me on this path toward a new religious concept for humanity. The contents of this material, I feel is the truth of which all mankind has been searching.

In his book "Messages to Mankind from the Almighty and His Spirits" Mr. Homics and others spoke directly with spirits about answers concerning religion, science (social and metaphysical) life, creation and the universe. In this book, I propose to show you what I have come to believe as the saving messages to humanity. Hopefully, you will see that the creative spirit in humanity has risen to a level where we can now understand the true aim and sense of life. This book will focus on the possibility of providing to those who feel a desire to understand life, and a clearer and better explanation of life and creation.

Revelation of the Truth

As I explored this religion, it became apparent to me that brotherhood, love, peace, justice, and prosperity were unobtainable with our current religious doctrines. Why was this so? This new religion teaches the idea of consolidating all of our present day religious beliefs into one ideal and understanding. This must be done so that all of the teachings of religion will be seen as one set of rules from God. This set of rules does not imply that any religious doctrine must eliminate or destroy their teaching; it simply means that this new religious revelation must become the building block for a better understanding of religion, creation, and life.

In coming to terms with this information, I learned that Gods envoys to earth did not teach religion on the basis of one being better than the other. In fact, the earth was filled with many nations of people who did not know of each other's existence. God sent messengers to each of these nations to provide to the people some knowledge about creation, life, and the universe. All the envoys provided information in relation to the traditions, customs, and limited knowledge of their immediate world.

It appears that God's objective was not to treat mankind to any opposition of thought regarding religion, but rather to give each nation some perspective of religion and His law to love one another. Also, God's concern was to determine whether the people of each nation were able to accept the new information, which was being provided. As a result, each nation s felt that the truth revealed to them is final and perhaps better than every other. Each nation ha resigned themselves to the idea that their prophet was divine. This is indeed the case; however, now we must look at why these prophets taught religion differently.

Four major religions were developed in India. Although no one knows who founded the Hindu religion, studies have shown that specific persons were responsible for reforming the doctrine of Hinduism. Nanak, who lived from A.D. 1469 to 1539, founded the doctrine of Sikhism in India. Two other founders of religious doctrines who lived in the sixth century B.C. gave new meaning to Hinduism as well. They were the Divine Vardhamana and Gautama. In the sixth century of China there were the religious founders Confucius, who founded Confucianism, and Lao-tzu, who founded Taoism. In what is now known as Iran, the prophet Zarathushtra founded Zoroastrianism. It is believed that Zarathushtra lived some time between 1400 and 1200 B.C., and this religion was founded in the Near East or Middle East, whereas Nataputta Vardhamna founded the Jainism religion and Siddhartha Gautama founded Buddhism some time in the sixth century B.C. n Asia. Judaism appeared in the sixth century B.C. as well. The prophets of this religious doctrine were Abraham, Isaac, Joshua, and Moses. They lived in the region of Canaan. The two most recent envoys of God are currently recognized today as Jesus and Muhammad. These two religious founders originated in the Middle East.

Let us take a glimpse into what each nation believed was intrinsic to its beliefs concerning the laws of life and nature. Each nation of people evolved in their own environment and every nation advanced according to their own particular culture and social practice. Each of their environments allowed for the use of natural materials to specific degree of enhancement.

Asian people were different culturally and therefore viewed life differently than African, European, or Mid-Eastern people. For example, the people who lived in the far interior of the African continent were not perhaps considered as sophisticated and refined as the people of Asia. Other ethnic groups thought other cultures were less civilized than their own. Therefore, Asian people, who had invented paper and ink with which to communicate and record history, were considered highly cultured while people living in the far interior of the African continent, using the method of memorized, storytelling, or drums to communicate or record their history, were not considered culturally advanced. But the common factor that has woven the very existence of humanity is the fact that God consider all human being as having the same need to know of His existence; therefore, each nation of people had to receive knowledge about God differently. Their particular envoys were able to express themselves based on the level of each nation's development. Contrary to the fact that each nation had to reach a level of mutual civilization and culture, it has to be seen that each nation received enlightenment on the basis of their attained knowledge. Each era in which the envoys revealed messages to their respective nations of people was different; therefore, it must be recognized that mankind had progressed beyond the ideals and knowledge of his predecessors in each of the succeeding eras of religious revelations. Let us not forget that the shaman, medicine men, and witch doctors of primitive cultures were also founders of religious doctrine. Although their religious doctrine may not be recognized as practical, it still has to be considered that all religions came about as a result of religious reforms and development, in terns of mankind's elevation culturally, socially, and technologically.

As mankind began to interact with different nations and cultures, the idea of religion changed as a result of different religious philosophies and ideologies interfacing with one another. Each religious founder was a messenger of God; the purpose of each envoy, however, was to relate an ideal that was pertinent to the people of their own time frame, culture and traditions. God is responsible for the development of His religious truth. Each of His envoys could only give to the people of their time the truth in terms of their nation's cultural and social development. As nations began to advance more in the knowledge of their world, God sent His envoys to help people come to understand more of the truth as it related to life, the universe, and religion.

Unlike other revelations given to us by God's envoys these new religious messages were revealed directly to ordinary human being. What was revealed did not come as a result of intuition, thought, or mysticism. These human beings found themselves in the midst of talking with spirits. These spirits included those that we recognize as envoys from ancient time, as well as the apostles of Jesus Christ. It is therefore the intention of God to give to us this new information, because we as human beings have grown to understand the world in the context of one meaning. Science has reached into the past of human existence and given us consistency as it relates to the evolution of the earth. Although humanity still draws a line between what science has revealed and what religion exclaims, the circle of convention needs to be connected. It is within this vein that these messages are being given to mankind. It is not expected of mankind to relinquish its current ideas concerning our religious views because, just as in ancient times, mankind must come to trust and believe these messages based on our ability to comprehend a new sense of reality. All of the founders of religion provided mankind with a new sense of direction and purpose for the development of humanity. These messages strive to give humanity a new understanding of spiritual life. It is expected that these messages will provide humanity with a catalyst by which it will create an improved society and world.

With this new information we will be able to deal concretely with the reality of life. God does not need to intervene with mankind by performing miracles to show us He exists, nor does He want to command humanity to follow this new religion. He only wants to see if humanity has risen sufficiently to understand this information. As humanity progresses, each new year has brought about doubt regarding faith in God and in His religious teachings. Man's faith is as uncertain as the vapors of fog. We have believed in the devil, hell, and the ultimate destruction of this plant; this new faith reveals, however, that man can and must take steps toward a new direction of understanding the purpose of our existence and how we came into existence. This religious concept explains life and the beginning of life in an entirely different way, and it also gives a different dimension to who and what God is and what He does for the living spirits of mankind.

This new religion shows that heavenly paradise does not exist as man has come to understand it. Although heaven exists it can now be understood that all human spirits come from heaven and their spirit will return there once the life of the body ceased to be. There is, however, no such place as hell.

In his book, Homics explains that, "When we are young children, fairy tales help explain to us our questions about life, ourselves, the world and other things. Later when we grow older we find the truth in books, schools, and from our parents who explain things differently.

"The same is true for mankind. Thousands and thousands of years ago the stories about our planet, the sun, the stars, etc., were different from the stories of today. Fairytale-like explanations or parables, as in the Bible and other books of religion, were needed to make people of long ago understand something of creation, life, etc.

"The time has come when man can understand more than that which he was told in his childhood, to many question he finds different answers than he got before. He is able to leave his footprint on another plant and use powers unknown to him before.

"When a father sees that his children are old enough to better understand real life, he tries to give them the right answers to questions, and they are different from those given to children when they are unable to understand."

"This is also what happened in the development of mankind. The Creator watched the development of humanity's civilizations. When the occasion arose that man needed to comprehend his world better, the Creator revealed different answers to questions concerning explanations of life and creation in a more comprehensive sense. The Creator sent to various nations of earth envoys to see if the people would listen and understand what was being revealed. As each nation of people came to understand the knowledge, the envoys revealed they considered the messages but understood them differently. Although most people agree that they came from the same source, they have until this day not agreed on the teachings of the envoys.

So, in order to end misunderstanding and mistakes as they are revealed in books of religion, such as the Bible, the Koran, the Vedas, and other religious books, the Creator has decided to reveal the truth directly to man. He has done this by speaking directly to spirits that were incarnated in human bodies and his high spirits that are not incarnated in human bodies spoke with these specially selected people. Everyone on earth has a right and an obligation to know and transmit this information to the rest of humanity. It is important that everyone understand the truth about creation, the universe, and life."

What these messages contain are the essential truths, which relate to a totally new understanding of life. Uncertainty looms in that which is new. These messages reveal to humanity an awareness relating to a new truth. The Creator of the universe has provided to mankind, through His chief spirits, knowledge about His will and His Religious laws.

Hopefully, this new religion will be questioned. Mankind must, however, first become acquainted with these new messages in order to ask relevant questions, because out of questions answers will come. Certainly not the answers we have become accustomed to, but new and different answers will illuminate the way toward a new pathways for the continued progress of humanity.

The most important questions, however, that come to mind are: Will mankind allow our reasoning to alter this new truth? Will mankind take this truth and move beyond our imposed concepts and notions about life, God, and ourselves? Will our reasoning be so set in stone preventing us from realizing that the days of religious allegories and parables are finished? In these messages lies the sweet fruit of truth.

To obtain peace, call not for the obliteration of mankind but rather for a new understanding of spiritual life and creation. This understanding will serve to illuminate the ways of love. The only rule by which we can overcome wars, greed, starvation, poverty, and hate is with the law of love. Also, we must gain faith in coming to acknowledge and comprehend our individual immortal spirit.

** All religions can and must become unified into one ideal or religious doctrine.

** No one religion is better than any other religion.

** Ancient religion as well as contemporary religions were provided to mankind so that human beings could kno something of creation, life, and the universe.

** God sent different envoys with new religious revelations to determine if the people were able to accept the new knowledge that was being provided.

** All religious revelations stem from the cultural and traditional development of the society or nation that received the messages.

** These new religious revelations were revealed directly to ordinary human beings (incarnated spirits in human bodies) by spirits that were not incorporated in human bodies.

Origins Of The Messages

In order to explain the origins of these messages, I must tell you a story. This is a story about the discovery of the messages and the people who originally received them.

Imagine if you will a person or a group starts on a journey and wanders into a lost land. Here they are in a land never explored and unknown. In this land they become trapped and unable to escape. While they look for some route of escape, they encounter explanations and reasons for questions concerning nature and life. From the answers discovered they were destined to be where they are, and they also find out that they must relay all that they have seen to all humanity. Upon their departure, however, they learn that the land they discovered will disappear. They must now tell everyone of their experience, but there is nothing left for them to use as proof that this land existed.

This is essentially what I feel has happened in the course of the Message Bearers receiving these messages. They started into the realm of the unknown. The original purpose of this journey was to get information about the future and possible potential fortunes. The Message Bearers were exploring the spirit world, trying to do as everyone else had tried and are still trying. They wanted to communicate with spirits to determine their fate in the world.

They were not what one would consider extraordinary people with clairvoyant capabilities; they were simple, ordinary people looking for some golden opportunities. In the midst of World War II these people were looking for a way to maintain stability within their lives. Their medium used to communicate with the spirits consisted of a round table, a circle of Latvian letters, and a saucer. With these items they were able to establish contact with the spirits and chronicle the information.

The entire method used to contact the spirits has not as yet been revealed. I have not been able to ascertain any information relating to how and what the Message Bearers did to contact the spirits. I am sure, however, that this information will be revealed at some time; what is important now is what has been revealed by the Almighty's spirits.

In reference to the Message Bears coming together, the story is as follows: The initial phase of the plan started with Mary and Lillian, who lived in the country of Latvia. During 1942 and 1944, Latvia was not involved in the war; however, they were still impacted by it. During this period, Mary and Lillian decided to try what was at that time a favorite preoccupation: contracting the spirit world. They channeled their thoughts to open the passageway for humans to communicate with the spirit world. Long before significant messages were given to these individuals, they kept attempting to contact the spirit world. With the same urgency that exists today, these individuals wanted to know if their fortunes would manifest in the future. I can imagine that their first efforts were painstaking.

Living in peace, they made attempts to remain secure, but then the Russian soldiers were coming closer to their doorsteps. They wanted desperately to find a way out of this situation as they were two women with homes and lives dealing with the potential threat of destruction their security.

They were perhaps before this time two logically thinking women, their lives carefree as they nestled in the daily routine of family life.

So, now you perhaps understand their desperation to get out of harm's way. They sought the abstract and unknown method of getting tangible results. Why not try talking with spirits? Others had done it throughout the course of human development. There has been and still is a segment of society who professes the capability to predict the future or talk with spirits in the spirit world.

We call them psychics, fortunetellers, and clairvoyants. In the same vein, these two women attempted to become psychics.

They called upon the spirits to speak, and they contracted Dagmara and Aurora. Mary, along with Alexander Upeniks, a close friend of Mary, struck up a casual conversation with these two spirits. Although Mary and Lillian had initiated this task long before anyone else participated, Lillian had lost interest after a while. Eventually Mary asked other people to participate.

Alexander at first was not interested in dealing with this little game, as he did not think anything would come of this activity. He simply thought of it as a way to humor Mary. It was also viewed as a way to while away some time, or do something of an obscure nature out of vague curiosity. However, just as any inventor or discoverer has shown, sometimes the insignificant can become significant. As time passed and this activity continued the participants of this obscure practice began to notice something somewhat peculiar. Alexander noticed that words were being spelled out in the Latvian language, utilizing logical Latvian words and phrases.

For some time this occurrence did not make any sense. Alexander, however, could no longer laugh at this occurrence;

he had to comprehend it. He wanted an explanation for what was happening. I can imagine sitting at a round table with a circle of letters and a saucer asking some questions to some unknown presence and getting a response. Each time the saucer indicated a letter to be written down, you would assume that some trick was being used and thus would take it less than seriously. But then to your amazement the reply would be in clear Latvian. Not only that, the answers would be different from what you had come to believe or know in reply to questions concerning creation, life and the universe. New secrets were being revealed about God, Satan, the Almighty, the Deoss Temple, the Solar and Lunar Fields. Subjects were discussed in a different, unheard of and in unimag- fined ways, as well as subjects concerning things that had until now been inexplicable. After a while, you would have to consider the merits of this occurrence. Would you continue or terminate these sessions and go on with your ordinary life? How do you test a phenomenon such as this? Here they were everyday ordinary people dealing with an occurrence of this magnitude.

You must also take into consideration that these spirits were not revealing information that Mary and Lillian wanted. The spirits did not answer questions pertaining to wealth and happiness. They simply answered question relating to life and the conditions of life. In others words, the who, what, where, when of the spirit world, and the why and what for of the man's world. Mary Mezins and Alexander Upenieks, who, as it turns out, was the person destined to be the senior member of the group, continued to receive these messages from the Almighty's chief and high spirits, as well as, Dagmara and Aurora. Each of the participants, who included Alexander Homics, the author of "Messages to Mankind," dealt with a power so immensely intense that while some could withstand the mental requirements to communicate with the Almighty's spirits, other could not. The people who made up the core group were Alexander Upenieks, Alexander (Alexo) Homics, John Kuzics, John (Janoss) and (Marija) Mary Mezins, Henry, Emily, and Nicholas.

That is all I know of the Messages Bearer, from out of obscurity came the messages, and these messages have remained in obscurity until now. The living survivors of the Message Bearers may give an account of what their lives were about, but as of this time, I have no knowledge of what their lives entailed.

Now we can talk about my involvement with discovering and attempting to disseminate these messages. To begin, le me try to describe who I am. First I must tell you that I am not a teacher or prophet sent by God to deliver these messages; I am certain that if God wanted someone in that category, He would have sent some one other than me. Over these past several years I have been an enigma to myself, as well as to everyone else. When I speak of being strange, however, I am speaking of it in the sense of purpose. What is my purpose, mankind's purpose, and anyone's purpose for being alive? I was looking for answers to life just like you are. Eventually however, the question became; who really knows? I have conjured up some pretty good answers in the process of discovering the truth, but invariably the truth was always the same and less true.

The truth is what you know and believe. Many times I crossed the pathways of different truths. They all seemed reasonable to me, yet I somehow remained confused. So I pieced together some ideas I considered important and dealt with my own truth. It was Mr. Homics' book that brought me to a point of clarity and understanding of a new truth.

The first volume of "Messages to Mankind From the Almighty and His Spirits" was published in 1976. The second volume was published in 1977. At the time of Mr. Homics' death, he had translated the rest of the material, another eight volumes, which remain unpublished. In 1992, Nick Mezins, son of John and Mary Mezins, published "Revelations: Extracts from The Book of Tidings of the Almighty and His Spirits to Humanity". Revelations summarizes highlights from the whole body of original materials, differing only in certain usages of the English language.

These messages have originated from something other than a religious occurrence. The cloud did not recede, nor did God speak in a thunderous voice. These messages were not even received in a church, temple, or synagogue, yet the origins of these messages are essential to the further growth and progression of humanity.

Goals Of This Book

In this book I hope to give to you knowledge concerning the messages that were received by the original Message Bearers. These messages are important and vital to my own existence. It is my hope that I will be able to convey to you how important and real these messages are to humanity.

This book offers new alternatives and explanations of life, and some may be difficult to accept or to conceive. I believe that this information will be accepted in the long term, but initially it may be difficult. My hope is that you allow this information to settle in your mind and not struggle to fully comprehend these messages in a familiar sense. I have taken the time to come to terms with this information so that I can, in turn, help others as they start on the path of understanding these revelations to mankind.

Let's say that you find a book containing what you might consider profound messages. What do you think would be the most difficult problem in interpreting and explaining the contents of the messages? From my own personal experience, the most difficult problem is not realizing that what you have discovered is actually the truth. Many times we resort to talking with people who know of our particular interest. In most cases, we gravitate and deal with people who have a compatible viewpoint. We talk with family members, teachers, associates, colleagues, and ministers. In my case, however, there was no one able to help me focus on my point of view.

I have written and rewritten this book for the past twenty-four years. I had no idea what I could say to convince others of this new faith. Since I have come to have faith in this new "religion", I feel certain that others will believe these revelations as well. Just as I gained faith in this information, others will have the opportunity to explore and come to terms with this information as well.

Nevertheless, this book will show you something different, providing answers to questions concerning our creation and the purpose of our creation.

These answers will be different from what has been told to humanity in the past as well as in the present. Hopefully, you will feel, as I have, that humanity has reached a level of confusion as it relates to the spirituality and the purpose of life. This book will attempt to explore and compare new as well as old ideas relating to the current philosophies of religion.

Essentially, this is a new religion, yet at the same time it deals with the same ideals that were established by our ancestors. In the course of coming to believe in this new faith I have had to dispel all previous notions of current religions. Even though this new religion has yet to be embraced as an established idea or principle, I recognize this faith as a new era of religion. I view myself as a new-age person, and so I want to offer others the opportunity to become the same. What I am attempting to accomplish in writing this material is an introduction to something that has become beautiful and wonderful to me.

For the most part, you will experience a sense of disbelief and at the same time a feeling of astonishment. You will discover a new purpose for living, and a new meaning for humanity's existence. This faith does not ask you to forsake your current religious beliefs, nor does it attempt to gain your faith by instilling fear or by offering a reward. This faith does not deal with the practice of showing a vengeful God who will destroy the world if people do not choose to believe in His word; this religion only wants to show what is the real truth to life. It deals with the same properties as all other religions; that is, to see if mankind has risen to a level where it can comprehend and accept the new information that is being revealed to it.

This religion does not require the destruction of our current religious institutions but rather requires that all religious institutions unite and consolidate into one faith. This religion comes as a means to supplement and supersede all current religious doctrines and beliefs. This religion gives to humanity an opportunity to once and for all unite in brotherhood, love, peace, and justice.

This new faith is not concerned with testing mankind's strengths or weaknesses; it is merely telling mankind of a religion that has existed since before the creation of this planet. It also gives mankind eliminating by the false conceptions imposed upon us by our ancestors. This this does and live, must he how into insight book will demonstrate how we must learn to cooperate and come to recognize our dual entities of body and spirit.

This material was written with the intent of showing our progenies that the world will not continue to live in fear and confusion. The basis tenet of all religions is that there is only one God. We must begin to teach our children that the values and principles taught by one religion are the same for all religions. My sincere wish is that this book will lead others in the direction of following a new path toward peace, love, and hope for all humanity.

The Almighty's spirits spoke with the Message Bearers to provide information to humanity, information to help humanity to start on the path toward creating an ideal and happy life, to direct humanity from the road of delusion on which it is currently traveling, to help humanity understand its errors and reveal to humanity who we are, the goals of human life, who our Creator is, the Creator's goal for creating our world, and to explain the Creator's religion for the entire universe. Mankind alone cannot get the answers to these questions by himself. Not even with the assistance of his genius mind will mankind be able to find out who God is and the spirits are, nor the essence, course and task of man's spirit both within the human body and outside of it. They explain the notion of good and evil, as well as reveal the truth about the Almighty's messengers, and religions on earth.

    This book will alter the course of human life and the develop ment of humanity. Peace will become a part of the human condition as opposed to a symbol of human desire and need. Here now we come to the point of recognizing a new spirit speaking to humans. You might experience a weird sense or feeling here because this spirit is omnipresent. Just as God's spirit is capable of being in many places at once so too are the high and chief spirits of the universe. It is at this point that your thoughts will be observed and monitored when you read any of the messages being spoken by them. This allows them to convey to The Almighty the direction by which we as human are deciding to go. We have a free will to choose to believe these Messages or allow them to fall into decay. In any event I know from experience that this can be a very unsettling feeling. It took me some time to get use to knowing that these spirits are still in existence and only want to see if mankind has grown sufficiently to comprehend these Messages.

Conversations with the Almighty Spirit

AURORA

(August 3, 1958)

"Heralds, after a long time I have once again come to you along with those who once were together with you on the estate. Yes, that was once, in the small two-story house, not far from old Riga, along the road to the seashore. Next to the house was a shed-a barn. If the door was open one could hear the neighing of the horses, the mooing of cows, the pleasant voice of the pigs, and of course the song of the rooster. Old trees protected the small house with their shade. A small brook slowly meandered past the house. The orchard pressed against the walls of the house, shoving the berry bushes.

"That was a house which was beloved by all of you, and it will remain dear for all time. At one time that house was important to you, it will be important to the entire world, because the first words of the messages were heard in it.

"Those whom you remember today-Alexandra and Nicholas-lived in it. Back when they lived in it, the house was like any other house. Only after mother and son had departed from it, in order to move to the splendid Castle of Heaven, did this house become the only one in the world in which for the first time could be heard the words of the Almighty's spirits. I was one of the first ones.

Now you have departed from this house and after long, arduous travels have found yourselves a new house on the ocean's other shore. Much has changed over these many years-in your life as well as in the world. These were times of war when we met for the first time, but neither is it a time of peace as we meet today. The world has ended the big war but it has not concluded a peace; it lives in the shadow of the third, the largest World War.

"Everyone is preparing for this war. Entire armies of specialists and scientists work for it. This work is intended for destruction, but in reality it is being done for the good of humanity's future. Without the pressures of this war, humanity would have spent many years in order to achieve what is being achieved in months. I can say that some very important things would have been discovered only after a long time, and perhaps even never.

"The new inventions cost so horribly much that without the pressure or the threat of war no one would risk spending these huge amounts of money. The cost of these inventions, though, no matter how great it may seem now, is trivially small compared to the good they may bring humanity.

"During this century man acquires wings. This year he starts to send self-Horde moons around the Earth. He hopes to reach the moon still this year and other planets after that. Obviously almost insurmountable difficulties stand in his way to other planets. But this-almost is dependent on human genius. How likely can that be? Man has achieved much that formerly seemed impossible. As a tiny part of the Almighty's spirit, man's abilities have in fact no set bounds. The only thing that could hold man back is the Almighty's will, which alone can also stop the Almighty Himself.

"Based on your invitation, I came today along with the spirits who were with you on Earth and whom you remembered over the last few days' to jointly recall the past, the present, and to jointly think about the future. We have accomplished that and the time has come to part again, with a beloved realization that the years have passed but that they have not carried off along with them the warning feelings of love and friendship which we and you will take along with us to heavens."

The conversations that took place with spirits, according to the Message Bearers as shown in the messages, reveal that all spirits have their own individual personalities. Each spirit spoke differently and in their own particular perspective. Some of the conversations with the spirits were very friendly, while others spoke tersely and sternly. Some of the conversations dealt with ordinary issues pertaining to the Message Bearers previous lives or private lives, while other conversations were concerned with revelations of life, religion, science, spirituality, and social conditions relating to society's needs.

Imagine if you will, talking with spirits. Spirits are immaterial so they do not have vocal cords or any such things as mouths. Spirits communicate through thought or mentally. Some spirits are capable of communicating with all spirits, such as chief spirits or superior spirits, while others can only communicate with other spirits who are of the same level or lower. It is not possible to hear any spirit's thought; a spirit must grant you permission to communicate with them. Spirits must advance through several stages before they reach the level of divine, when a spirit obtains eternal individuality.

The spirits have to pass through the entire Lunar Fields, and the Solar Fields before they essentially enter the Deoss

Temple. Those who feel that they may not have what it takes to proceed to the level of divinity may decline it and stay in the thirteenth circle of the Solar Field eternally. This is no disgrace, but does prevent them from the possibility of eventual advancement. Others have to struggle hard and for a long time before they achieve the level-or degree-of divinity. There are thirteen levels that a spirit must achieve in order to become an eternal spiritual entity. A spirit has to ascend or advance through the thirteen levels of the Lunar Fields and then complete twelve levels of the Solar Fields before starting towards the level of divinity. A spirit may elect to stay in the thirteenth circle of the Solar Field, wherein they will be assured of eternal existence. However, those spirits that start towards the degree of divinity can still pass into non-existence. That can only happen if the spirit makes a serious mistake to merit non-existence. No spirit has, as yet, reached the level of divinity; however, the spirit of Alexander Upenieks has come closest to reaching that level. The spirits that spoke to the Message Bearers were at various levels in relation to their existence. The chief or superior spirits are so close to the Creator that they can be considered different personalities of Him.

When I first began to read the messages I often felt the presence of the spirit that was speaking in the book. You must understand that the spirits did not simply vanish after these messages were revealed-they are still in existence. Therefore, when you read what they said to the Message Bearers you can conceivably relate to an actual voice, almost like playing a tape, CD, or listening to the radio. The presence of the spirits speaking is like listening to them speaks mentally.

On many occasions I let other people read the original source. When they read "Messages to Mankind from the Almighty and His Spirits," they would exclaim that it was either "black magic" or the work of some evil force.

Everyone who tried to read the messages was frightened and figuratively threw the book back to me.

Initially I would read these Messages at night when there was nothing to distract me. Although I never communicated with the spirits directly, I felt their presence each time I read the messages. I have picked out a few passages dealing with these messages and, for the most part, I have used segments that deal with the superior or chief spirits speaking. The superior or chief spirits speak with urgent authority; they do not talk of issues that can be considered general or informal. Their intonation may be considered offensive or perhaps arrogant. But consider, if you will, the fact that they have a responsibility to the entire universe. When they spoke with the Message Bearers they did so with a specific purpose, and had no intent to consider how they felt regarding their intonation. Perhaps you can compare them with your father or mother. When your parents spoke to you about serious matters, more than likely they used a tone that denoted the seriousness of the matter being discussed. They didn't cover up their conversation with frivolity; they made their point and hoped you understood. If you didn't, the consequences for not comprehending were your problem. The same applies to the spirits and their conversations with the Message Bearers and now with you. As you read the conversations, you must picture yourself in contact with the spirits or the spirits in contact with you. In the course of providing this information, I will quote passages dealing with various topics that were discussed with the Message Bearers. I will include the name of the spirit that spoke, and the date that the conversation took place. I will be dealing specifically with issues concerning creation, God, Satan, and the spiritual world, as well as worldly issues, such as mankind's tasks, duties, and responsibilities to the human race.

Most of the spirits' conversations I will quote are dealing with spirits of a high degree. In actuality these spirits are the ones whose functions are just as important as God. You will come to know that all spirits are assigned different tasks and duties. Some of the spirits have been around for hundred of millions of years. You will also discover that time is relative in the spirit world, and that all spirits can live eternally. Spirits are immortal.

As you may see, the spirit Aurora's conversation with the Message Bearers is as if they were talking on the telephone. Although there wasn't any physical means of communicating, Aurora was able to speak as a human through mental contact. This friendly conversation also provided some important information as it relates to mankind's status at that time and in the future.

The first conversations dealt mainly with information concerning life of the spirits and their human counterparts. These conversations are not meant to scare or frighten anyone; rather, they are meant to elevate the human being to a position of recognizing their spiritual entity. As we continue I hope that you will comprehend what the spirits have to say. Please do not judge their conversation on the basis of human emotion but rather on the premise that they do not exhibit emotion, and are speaking within the realm of their authority. Their conversation will only serve to enlighten you to the nature and will of the superior spirits and the Creator of the universe.

I will attempt to give you an example of what I am trying to say. When leaders of nations want to have their rules or laws acknowledged by the general population, they usually designate someone to carry out this task. The person assigned the duty of promulgating the decision of the leader has to deal with the specific information, not the attitude of its recipients. I have on occasion watched the news and have seen a spokesperson speaking with the press concerning various situations. During the Gulf War, for example, the spokesperson for the State Department kept the press apprised of the needs and decisions of the government. Although the spokesperson may not have been involved in the decisionmaking process, he was still able to brief the press and the citizens of the U.S. with respect to the continuing development of a given situation.

The spirit's conversations are somewhat similar to that of a spokesperson: they are assigned the task of speaking to humanity. The Almighty, God, and Satan have designated certain spirits to speak with mankind and their duty is to spread the information that the Almighty and His superior spirits want mankind to know. There is much to reveal, so I will leave it up to you at this point to draw your own conclusions.

** The spirits that conversed with the Message Bearers were of various levels with differing personalities.

** The conversations dealt with mankind's need to have questions answered concerning life, creation, religion, science, spirituality, and social conditions as they relate to society's needs.

** The spirits spoke to the messages Bearers mentally. Because the spirits are not materials in nature, they do not have vocal cords or mouths.

** The superior or chief spirits spoke with urgent authority.

** The spirit Aurora was one of the first spirits to converse with human beings or the Message Bearers mentally.

** As previously mentioned, the conversations are meant to elevate the human beings to a position of recognizing their spiritual entity.

A Question of Faith

In the course of mankind's development we have progressed to a point where nations are no longer separated. Humanity possesses the power to communicate, travel, and store vast amounts of information, allowing him to understand other cultures, societies, governments, and people, each of which differs as sunlight to night. Yet why have we, as a single race of people, not realized our commonality? Isn't the dark of night as useful as the sunlight of day? The two elements share a common purpose. One allows for people to work and enjoy the benefits of life while the other allows reprieve or rest from the daily toil of work and recreation. Just as they differ but share a commonality of purpose, so do the races of mankind.

Many people believe that God needed mankind to suffer and feel pain in order to prove that we love Him. Why was it necessary? For example, it is said that Jesus died on the cross for our sins, and in so doing suffered the bitter brutality inflicted on Him by man. But, I asked myself over and over again; didn't Jesus want to save mankind from punishment and suffering? Didn't God send Him to Earth to teach humanity about love and salvation? The story is written that we must believe in the Holy Spirit of Jesus Christ, but how many of us realize or recognize our own spiritual entity?

Another example is based in a much younger faith. Many of you may have heard of extra-sensory perception. I was on a Greyhound bus bound for my destination with fate. I had, however, become so spellbound with religion that I wanted to test my faith with someone. I looked across the aisle and there was a perfect subject for me to try out my new found faith: there in the seat a couple of feet away from me sat a middle-aged woman. She appeared to be an ordinary person, her clothes were simple, she wasn't wearing makeup, and she had in her possession a Bible. I thought to myself; if you believe in God, touch your nose. I was transmitting the thought to her, but I didn't motion or attempt to alert her to my presence. As a matter of fact, her eyes were closed and she was in a state of semi-sleep. I kept on repeating in thought, "if you believe in God touch your nose". I continued this thought for several minutes, and suddenly she opened her eyes and looked directly into mine. We had made contact mentally.

Somehow we had established contact, but I still did not react to her verbally. I just continued to think, "if you believe in God touch you nose". After several attempts she looked at me in a very strange and curious manner and attempted to avoid my glance, but I persisted in my unusual form of communication. Eventually, the lady touched her nose. Of course, I was sure my mental communication had caused this action, so with enthusiasm I got out of my seat bounding toward this woman. Her only reaction toward me was that I might be a demon or a disciple of the devil coming to get her. Her prayers rang forth for the Lord to help her: "Get this man off of the bus," she exclaimed. No one knew her reason for becoming hostile toward me, as no one had seen me do anything to her. She got off the bus at the next stop. I have never been able to get this episode out of my mind. I thought for a long time that I might possess ESP; however, I was never able to perform the same feat again.

After I had read the Messages several times I reflected on that incident and asked myself, Could it have been that I used my spiritual entity to communicate with that woman? The Messages illustrated to me, as hopefully they will show you, that there exists two separate but distinct bodies which inhabit one another: the spirit, which is manifested by the Almighty, and the body, which is manifested through man. These Messages allowed me to understand the truth of reincarnation, and how it has affected man's growth and development. We will look at the question of life and death in a later chapter in which case the matter of reincarnation will be discussed in more detail.

I am certain that you know mankind's vision has been directly responsible for our growth and development. In our quest for knowledge we have conquered; in our restlessness we have made discoveries and built out of them the foundation for civilization; in our desire to rise above the clouds we have soared; in our pursuit for knowledge we have acquired intellect, and yet our spirits still remain restless. Mankind's pursuit for knowledge has left many people deprived of the ability to utilize, participate, or contribute to the development of life and society. In our effort to conquer the unknown, we have suppressed and oppressed the majority of people to a limited knowledge of life and creation. But why?

One answer is that mankind does not know of its true spiritual entity. We have identified with just being human: flesh, bones, and blood only. For centuries we have blindly pursued and translated as truth what can now be considered fairy tales and parables left by our ancestors. Our religious beliefs expound the fact that we must believe in the laws of God. But ask yourself: is mankind in its entirety benefiting from God's law? Perhaps you can say yes, but there are others who will disagree with you.

I have discovered in reading the Messages that religion in its truest form serves only to enlighten, strengthen, and develop man to understand his aim and purpose and to carry out the will of his Creator.

Our creator wants us to comprehend why He created life, not just command the existence of life for His personal pleasure-that is why we must continue to exist, and have continued to exist on this planet and in the universe. As long as poverty persists, wars continue, and devastation and destruction prevail in the world, it must be concluded that the laws of God are not being followed. Our ancestors interpreted the laws of God, but why is mankind still so far removed from having peace and tranquility within society? Somehow, we must look closely at the direction that mankind is traveling; we must acknowledge that an "immunity" has built up within our society against the laws of God. People are more concerned with their own personal acquisitions. People want to have power and material wealth and they come to rely on having these things to overcome despair and suffering. They feel that wealth will shield them from the daily ordeal of human suffering. Those who can't obtain these physical possessions feel that God doesn't exist at all.

God does not enforce His laws, He merely gives us the laws and we must find ways to implement them. The way to establish institutions on earth, which will carry out the will of God, is through deeds and actions alone. It is not done by thinking God will somehow intervene at the appropriate moment and save the world from destruction nor will He destroy the world. I have learned that these Messages will help mankind build the ideal world, which the Creator wants. Paradise is mankind's destiny. The only thing we have to do is create it by obeying the law of God and that law is to love each other. The ideal world is one in which humanity is striving to obey the law of God. We are obeying God when we strive to eliminate poverty, hunger, selfishness and greed. We can come to terms with the law of God when we can recognize that our spiritual growth is more important than our material possessions on earth. The Messages show that the spirit is immortal and therefore more important than the mortal body.

** Humanity's growth and development is responsible for allowing us to recognize our commonality as humans.

** Mankind must come to recognize its physical and spiritual commonality.

** Mankind must not only recognize the blood and flesh of themselves but also their spiritual entity as a reality.

** The Creator has given mankind an opportunity to come to term with its new knowledge about life and the aims and sense of humanity.

** Spiritual growth is more important than material posses sion. The spirit is immortal and the body is mortal and there fore will die and decompose, while the spirit will continues to live eternally.

** Mankind must implement institutions that will carry out the will of God rather than waiting on God to fulfill His own laws given to man to obey.

The next spirit to speak to mankind is the superior spirit Santorino. Santorino is the spirit responsible to the inhabitants of our planet and the planet Earth itself. God has given Him the responsibility to help the spirits in their development and growth on our planet. He can be considered the guardian spirit of Earth. Listen to what He has to say concerning man's development and understanding of God:

Questions About God

SANTORINO

(January 6, 1967)

"Messengers to humanity on Earth, I come to you in the assignment of the Creator and guide of the world, and of the God of your galaxy, in order to convey to you the decisions of the High Rulers.

"The twentieth century draws to a close. Almost two thousand years have passed since Christ brought God's faith to Earth. Millions of years had to pass before humanity became capable of accepting the new true faith.

"Having originated along with the other animals, man did not differ from them for a long time. Yet, once he began to differ, the habits of animals still controlled him. He had furiously fought the other animals for his place on Earth. Many of them, much stronger than he, attempted to destroy man, but man won. Thanks to his intellect, he became the strongest animal on Earth.

"Initially, he invented gods for himself, because he needed a master and a guide. He considered God as someone still higher than his ruler. He called God his master and king. One God, however, was not enough for him: not only did he fill the Heaven with gods, but the earth and sea as well. They were called gods, but their spiritual qualities were the same as those of people. They were merely mightier than people.

"Humanity developed slowly. The time came to proclaim the meaning of the true God, who He was, what He wanted from man, and what man must be like. Prophets, people with highly gifted spirits, [incarnated in human bodies] came to people. The Ten Commandments came into existence; ten laws which express the will of God. These laws commanded what man must and must not do, yet these had been given to a man who had barely stood up firmly on his own two feet, one who still had a lot to learn and understand, as well as learn how to improve life. Thus humanity received God's highest envoy, sent to proclaim to humanity its highest law, the law of love. It is not force, the sword, or heroism that can lead man to a true, happy life on Earth.

"The words of Christ were simple and understandable to everyone. He brought love to man, and a happy future dependent on it. Man crucified Him, though, and continues to crucify for over a thousand years. The road of the Christian faith was a difficult one, because it was difficult for man to change his nature, which was formed over hundreds of thousands of years through constant battles and wars.

"The apostles were replaced by their successors, the disciples, and the disciples by other successors. The trade of priesthood developed. Yes, it was a trade! They wanted to rule and guide humanity, as it would be better for themselves personally. They enacted their own laws. Next to God and His angels, they placed the King of Hell, Satan, with His numerous legions of devils. They made the devil mightier than God. Since the words of Christ did not allow them to act as they were, they used a foreign language that no one understood in order to keep the words of Christ from the people.

"The English burned at the stake the first man who dared to translate the Bible into a language that was understandable to everyone." [William Tyndale in 1536]

"In order to save people from the power of the devil, the priests themselves became more horrible than the imagined devil. In order to protect God, they tortured people mercilessly and burned them at the stake. That sounds unbelievable, but that's the way it was.

"In lieu of Christ's teachings, they introduced innumerable prayers in the church, even though Christ insisted that this not be done. They implemented the confession of sins, and took money for that. They built palaces for themselves, while people lived in hovels. They held lavish banquets, while others were dying of starvation. They also tried to halt the development of sciences.

"You will claim that those were delusions: I, however, will say that it was a crime and the betrayal of Christ.

"The road of humanity is unstoppable, though. Printing of the Book of Holy Scriptures in a language understandable to people and its reading in churches had to be permitted. The church lost its secular power, and began to approach the demands of Christ's teachings.

"Yet, whenever an unjust power collapses, the people who have been liberated, having lost faith in the old, go too far and begin to deny the very existence of God.

"Thus came the time for the Almighty to give humanity a broader notion of Himself, the gods, and His goals and demands.

"There were times when it seemed that nothing good would come of humanity, and that the Almighty would give up on it. However, that did not occur and humanity, if not in its full entirety, at least to a great extent, began to travel the right road.

By giving up the normal forms of faith, many fell into extremism, and being unable to discern God, claimed that He didn't exist at all, or else, that God had died. Yet, who then had created this ungraspable world, including these entire animals and plant kingdom on Earth? Did everything come about by itse? That, after all, was more difficult to understand and more incomprehensible to, grasp than the existence of God." (Mezins 1992, pp. 363-365)

Humanity calls upon God daily to redeem our souls and forgive us of our sins, yet we continue to sin, constantly asking for God's grand intervention to save us from ourselves. Humanity is convinced that God will save us from ourselves; the majority of human beings and religions are convinced that God will save or destroy us. But where are the religious doctrines and orientations for our current and future generations? Is the present generation convinced, as many are, that God is coming to save this world? Where, in fact, do we stand on this long path of human evolution? We have envisioned the coming of God to save the human race. As the nature of humanity slips beyond our grasp, we are still asking God for His divine intervention.

We now stand on the threshold of a new awareness, a new awareness for all who have questioned the possibility or probability of God's existence. It is also for those who have faith that God exists. Mankind has reached a point where it does not need God for material support. We no longer have to travel by foot or other outmoded means of transportation. We can fly higher than any bird; we can communicate with anyone anywhere in the world. The miracles of man's inventions have made it possible to do all of the things that our ancestors could only dream of or pray for God to do, so why do we still need God?

I believe that mankind was not created as we are told, spontaneously out of the earth, nor were we created out of circumstances which relate to just the natural order of physical science or of mother nature. So the question becomes: what and who is that creative entity in actuality? A simple answer, if I were to believe that God is the only ruler of this universe. I, like many others, could satisfy my need to know more about creation and life if I endeavored to study only what has been revealed about such matters. Other questions, however, plague my mind, questions like: how did this superior being decided to create the universe and life? Why did He create human beings? How does He expect human beings to rule His created world? Why didn't the envoy teach us about the world as we have come to understand it? What is religion as it relates to each of its religious founders? From what source did the religious founder teach religion? There are a number of religious books with different answers to these questions, but which is correct?

Buddha, Indra, Mohammed, and Christ gave to mankind a realization of something greater than we are capable of learning from our natural cognitive process. They taught mankind of someone who existed, but this entity was invisible, unreachable, untouchable, and intangible. So why did mankind come to have faith in Him;

Before I discovered the Messages, I imagined that life was due to some extraordinary principle of nature. When I looked at a forest, or felt a gust of wind, I wondered how these things came into existence. Surely there had to be some explanation other than God just saying let there be this or that! Why was it that God could spontaneously create an entire universe, a planet with inhabitants, and laws to follow, yet there was no peace in the world? The universe follows specific laws: there is gravity, inertia, and the natural laws of nature, and nothing and no one can change these laws.

Yet the very laws that were given as instructions to mankind by God's envoys were not being obeyed. God said to love your fellow man, to share and to cooperate with him. He commanded for us to come together in harmony, peace, and unity. For centuries, however, mankind has yet to reach a state of brotherhood and peace. How can we go on believing in God if He doesn't somehow enforce His commandments? Does He really exist?

In today's world I witness our children having similar doubts and questions. They have reached a point where they just don't care about our religious beliefs or God. Who is to blame? Is it God's or mankind's fault? Who is responsible for shaping a person's view, as well as our children's faith about religion and God? Furthermore, how can we shape their view if we are not doing as God has commanded? We can't prove to them that God exists, but we can prove that His law of love can and must work for all humanity.

The truth of the matter is that it is not a question of whether or not God exist, but rather whether God has maintained His faith in mankind. Each day when I read newspapers or turn on the T.V. I read or hear of new atrocities and destruction happening in the world. It would be so wonderful if as prophesied by the Bible God returned and stopped the encroachment of man's pestilent against humanity, but because this hasn't happened, mankind goes forward looking for relief from his own created hell. Has God viewed all that has happened and is currently happening in our world and considered us unworthy of His intervention? Has man strayed so far away from the laws of God that He is allowing us to destroy ourselves?

We must now come to understand that it is because of God's belief in mankind that we continue to grow, to come together in peace, harmony, and unity. God gives to us the answers about life only when we have demonstrated to Him that our sense of struggle and suffering requires Him to give us further instructions and directions. The test of man is not only in his faith and belief, but also in his ability to change and develop beyond the conceptions of his thoughts. Man is the perpetuation of life and it is through his own actions and deeds that he saves himself. God has given us that responsibility. We are not required to praise God, nor will our praising Him bring about a change in our living conditions. It is not right to assume that God will allow us to understand more of ourselves only after we have convinced Him of our faith in Him; the Messages represent the fact that God wants us to understand a new truth. Will we understand it, or allow this new truth to suffocate in the trenches of blind faith and allegiance? I believe that the determined spirit within man will rise above the entity of himself and find his true destiny. This book will help you learn that eternal life lies not beyond the realm of Earth, but right here on Earth.

Humanity will begin to go further and progress beyond the imposed concepts and notions of past religious beliefs. God has once again given to mankind new answers concerning life and the creation of life, only this time the answers are not covered with myths and miracles, but are natural and real. No longer is the medicine of truth diluted with sweetness as for children, but now, as adults, it can be taken purely and naturally.

** Mankind has developed and evolved to a level where it can understand new religious information.

** Humanity has evolved beyond the level of its primitive ancestors to a point where we can understand more about God and His laws.

** Our primitive ancestors created gods for themselves, there by making gods of the natural elements, which did not benefit humanity.

** The gods of early man were nothing more than rulers that were imagined beings higher than their counterpart human rulers.

** God sent His envoys to Earth to teach the true meaning of His laws to mankind.

** Humanity received God's highest envoy (Jesus Christ) to proclaim to humanity His highest law: the law of love.

** The law of love was replaced with man's inventions for the trade of priesthood.

** The time came when the Almighty gave to humanity a broader notion about Himself, the gods, and His goals and demands.

* * The test of mankind is not only through his faith and belief of God, but also in his ability to change and develop beyond the conception of his thoughts.

** Mankind has the responsibility to save himself and society from his own menace and destruction.

** God's faith in mankind and man's need for knowledge has given humanity new information to help in understanding man's spiritual immortality and material mortality (body).

Questions About Science and Religion

For years there have been constant debates concerning the beginning of the world and the creation of man. Religion asserts one thing, while science insists on something else. Religion tells us to believe in the Bible and other books of religion, while science implores us to believe in empirical proof.

Let's look briefly at some of these inconsistencies as they relate to religion and science. God created earth and human in six days. Man however, evolved to his present form after several hundred million years, and started as a one-celled animal from the sea. The earth formed from molten rock and not from a single command of "let there be earth." The earth revolves around the sun as rather than a single command of "let there be a sun for day and a moon for night." Which is the truth? For centuries we have only seen God as the creator of life. If there was a question regarding God, which I fear many would consider blasphemous, we have only the past revelations with which to prove His word. But how is it that the world has not come to see God as one entity in His word and truth?

Let us say that man has prospered in his knowledge of science and technology. Has he benefited by his deeds to improve this world? Is the prosperity of man only to benefit those who provide others with the knowledge of their own convictions? In other words, have the "chosen" become stagnant in the trenches of greed, lust, and piety, and have lost sight of serving the cause of goodwill and prosperity for all humanity? Hasn't the common man labored enough with his strength and fortitude throughout these countless centuries to help construct systems that would provide them with their basis life needs? Through a torturous hell they have refortified these trenches with their love and trust in God and peace, but their suffering continues. The great Inquisition, the Crusades, the Magna Carta, the French Revolution, the American Revolution, The American Civil War, World Wars I and II, the Civil Rights Movement, and other historic moments denote the fact that mankind has ever so valiantly claimed the right to live as free and God-loving people, yet our freedom has been stymied because we have to deal with ambiguous answers of life and creation.

Comparing what is being taught by our religious leaders and scientists, what would be the major difference concerning their explanation of creation and life? From 1859, when Charles Darwin introduced the idea that all species of mankind were related and that mankind evolved over many centuries, scientists have sought to verify this assumption. Sketches have been drawn in the minds of people concerning the development of man. Louis Leakey, Raymond Dart, and others have allowed man to view the evolutionary stages of mankind. In their discoveries they have provided mankind with evidence that supports the evolutionary development of man from the state of Ramapithecus to his current state of modem man or Homo Sapiens. We can certainly acknowledge that man has undergone a wonderful transformation. Science has given man an impression of his unique adaptation to his environment and status. Scientists however, often place the value of man's progression on the development of his brain, whereas man's unique qualities are his hands and brain. These two components were compared with other animals, as time permitted man to examine the world and himself. Scientific investigations revealed that man's brain increased in size as mankind evolved to his present day existence. Scientists, therefore, have placed the burden of man's growth on the brain's ability to assess and evaluate, as to how man continues to progress.

Scientists conclude that because man endeavors to walk erect and make tools that this somehow allowed for the increase in man's brain size. They theorize that the first apes utilized their anus and hands, thus having the physical capabilities and the potential brain capacity to change themselves and their environment. The question then becomes: why did some apes acquire the will and desire to come out of the trees? Jane Goodall in her work showed that chimpanzees, man's closest relation, are still tool-users today. They throw rocks and branches, and use implements to find food, dig for food, clean themselves, and to drink water. They make tools and keep them in their possession. Other apes have similar traits and characteristics, yet they are still apes. Why? Was it just a larger brain, hand-in-hand development, improved manual dexterity, or something else that helped mankind to evolve and progress to his current state? Religion denies the empirical data that has been drawn from man's curious nature. Many religious people assert that life came about as a result of God's direct intervention. In religious fervor priests and ministers agree on this concept without question, and anyone of the Christian faith will not oppose this belief. In fact, for centuries this has been the Christian follower's only truth with which they have allowed themselves to confess.

Neither the religious leaders nor our scientists have been able to stay consistent with their beliefs or theories; they have had to constantly contradict their own beliefs. What was true and proven by their predecessors 2,000 or 200 years ago is not believed today, or at least the truth has been changed to address the current need of civilization, because different discoveries have led to new understandings. Hopefully, the discoveries of these Messages will serve to enlighten mankind as to what they can now confirm as the truth regarding mankind's evolution and creation. As millions of people read the Bible, Koran, and scientific journals, they conceivably widen the gap between imagination and reality. We must come to understand the fact that only the Creator of life can account for the creation of the universe and life. It is when He reveals information to mankind about how He created circumstance in the universe that resulted in the creation of life that we know of creation and its purpose. Therefore, mankind must see that with the overlapping of cultures, civilizations, and knowledge mankind has drawn a conclusion of knowledge about life and creation based of his accumulated information. Each succeeding generation has contributed to mankind's knowledge. Much of what the religious leaders' information consisted of was a belief in something that had been passed from one generation to next, and these beliefs were based on the information that was provided by our Creator. The belief had to be maintained because there was no other way of determining the truth except through belief and faith. The circumstances, however, were different for scientists. The early explorers of science took a different path: they sought to establish proof of life, as it existed. Questions began to appear within the minds of people: If the earth is not flat, then what is it? If I can see the external universe, then why am I consigned only to this planet? How is it that God created this entire universe and wishes only that I obey Him and never doubt or investigate His created world? Why is it that I can never say without the sanction of God and His priest on earth that which can be proven and shown? Scientists were drawn to assert their minds and go beyond the regimen of the church. Their discoveries are a compilation of tests, examinations, evaluations, and conclusions based on million of years of research. The first man who sought to understand the element of fire and learned how to control this substance was in fact a primitive scientist. Although the people of his tribe and the medicine men may have had doubts concerning his thoughts and goals, they were eventually convinced that what he discovered would be beneficial to them. These people we call primitive had within their society primitive scientists who discovered new ways for mankind to live, and as such science continues today.

Certainly by listening to both the religious leaders and scientists something of value can be learned and applied to life's situations; however, they have done little to improve the state of mankind's knowledge of his beginning and its purpose. The Messages will serve to assist religion and science to collaborate in unity and cooperation concerning the creation of life and the universe. It can be acknowledged that religion and science work from different premises, but both serves the needs of humanity. One deals with proof while the other deals with faith alone. One relates to the fact that there must be a reason why the universe exists, while the other confirms this reason through ethereal means. Nevertheless, each body of persons was created with the same purpose in mind: one, to explore the regions of the unknown, and the other: to give faith in what is unseen. The creative spirit of each group is endowed with the Creator's spirit; therefore, mankind moves forward as a result of knowledge and faith. You will come to see, as a result of learning these messages, that religion and science are interrelated and therefore able to lead humanity towards its destination with fate in harmony, peace, and unity. The superior spirit Santorino discussed it with the Message Bearers and said the following:

SANTORINO

(May 1, 1944)

"MIGHT SCIENCE AND RELIGION BE UNITED? No. Science is handling things that can be investigated; at least, they might be understood and proved. Religion asks you to believe without proof. Both of them also have something in common. They are: 1)

Understanding of the world; 2) investigation of the unknown; 3) striving to give mankind a better life; 4) trying to rid humankind of physical and mental suffering; 5) looking into eternity.

"As long as science is unable to answer all of its questions, it is helpless to satisfy the thirst of a human being for omniscience and peace of mind. This can only be given with religion.

"Scientists, looking into endless space of the universe, are trying to find there a supreme cause God. Not finding Him there, they will try to explain Him with the help of their minds and their scientific instruments. With these they will try to explain the Almighty. But with these things alone, it is impossible to explain the Almighty. They will not find Him. You cannot put the rays of the sun into an iron box and bring them into a laboratory to be studied under a microscope. You cannot not stop the wind to look at it. "What is it? " The wind will be nothing. You will be only able to ascertain that the wind is nothing or that it is something mystical. The rays of the sun and the wind should be investigated in different way-

Let us leave to science the explanation of everything that is on Earth. And how much capability does its telescopes have to reach into space? So the Almighty and the world of the spirits have to be left to religion. This is revealed by the Almighty Himself and through His spirits and me." (Homics 1976, pp. 119-120) (Mezins 1992, pp. 34-35)

** For centuries there have been contradictions between reli gion and science about the beginning of life and the universe.

** Religions give mysterious answers to the questions con cerning the beginning of life, while science provides answers, which can be tested and proven.

** Neither our religious leaders nor our scientists have been able to stay consistent with their answers due to the develop ment of humanity's societies and cultures.

** The Messages give credence to the ideas, which each group espouses concerning life and creation.

** Both groups have been responsible for mankinds knowl edge and condition on this planet. They both have sought to help mankind to understand the world, research the unknown, strive to give mankind a happy life, try to rid mankind of physical and mental suffering, and achieving a state of para dise and understanding immortality.

** Although they are trying to achieve the same things, they are essentially different: science can explain everything within the parameters of the physical plane on earth, while religion explains everything within the domain of the spirit world.

Questions About Ourselves

WHY ARE WE AS HUMANS COMPELLED to believe that only God can save us, and we do not consider the greater possibility of saving ourselves? The great envoys sent to this earth by God taught our ancestors. Jesus, Buddha, Confucius, and other great prophets taught mankind to believe in God and the spirituality of our being. The immortality that has been the salvation we have sought for centuries resided in the knowledge of complying with God's Commandments, yet in today's world we still witness destruction, devastation, deprivation, and world discord. Our lives are gripped with horrors and deeds of devastation that know not the bounds for the compassion of humanity. We stand listless and vulnerable to the hapless plight of all humankind, and we watch in dismay at the suffering caused by those who are selfish and greedy. The yoke of oppression restlessly and repugnantly restricts us from choosing the pathway to eternity, freedom, and justice. In our desire to be resurrected in God's truth and His light, we abstain from doing on earth what we do in Heaven, yet, in all fairness; mankind does address these social problems in our society. It is shown daily in mankind's actions and deeds that we try to help the poor and impoverished. People volunteer their time and make monetary contributions to charitable causes. We have a government in America that deals with the needs of its people. However, the circumstances of poverty are not being eradicated. More and more of our children are turning to anti-social behaviors. Our prison systems continue to expand, and there are more than enough people to accommodate the empty prison cells. Crime seems to decline and rise depending on the condition of our economies. Knowledge, however, continues to be sold at the expense of the unknowledgeable. Education of the masses is regulated by the ability of one to afford the cost for an adequate education, so educational systems differ from one jurisdiction to the next. When mankind can seriously see that the disparity between the so called "classes" is creating this sense of discontent within society then it will be the responsibility of all humanity to bring about a redistribution of all mankind's resources for the good of all humanity.

Up until now, religion has been a constant belief and knowledge concerning a truth revealed by a teacher sent by God, thereby creating a foundation for the development and perpetuation of religious institutions established on the principles of providing goodwill for all of mankind. Somehow we must begin establishing a contemporaneous attitude and knowledge in relation to religion. The preponderance of nations and governments are established on principles inconsistent with the religious truth we know and believe. The strength of mankind resides in knowing the truth, or of a truth. We, however, must comprehend that with the evolution of mankind came the evolution of knowledge. This fact has helped us examine and reexamine our convictions and beliefs, motivating us toward a greater consciousness and sense of direction. Each religious revelation has given us some understanding of religion, and all religions have made it possible for mankind to stay on a path toward a greater comprehension of life and the circumstances of living.

In our society we have many religious institutions that profess to have the truth and knowledge of who the Creator is and how He created life, but as we examine these truths we find that they all relate to past revelations that have been passed from one generation to the next. Century after century we have studied these revelations and established stability and credibility within the framework of religion and society. With the accumulation of knowledge and religions, however, certain inconsistencies have begun to appear regarding the truth of creation and life. Our present day religious leaders tell us to never question the truth as revealed by God, but if we take a closer look at what man has accomplished, we would find that what God has created, from the beginning with the Garden of Eden, has always been questioned. Because of these questions, new discoveries and inventions have only served to benefit mankind.

Society's religious institutions provide man with knowledge concerning a belief about God, so every nation has been given a glimpse of God. Every nation has established their belief on what was revealed to them by an envoy sent by God and has thus heard a story concerning God's existence. Also, every nation wants to believe that God will provide for them; they each pray for God to grant them peace, love, harmony, and everlasting life. Most of humanity prays for justice, brotherhood, and equality. Thousands of years have passed, and envoy after envoy has revealed the rules and laws of God, yet for many the question still remains: who, what, and where is God? If God exists, why have horrors, terrors, wars, and destruction continued? Humanity has prayed one thousand times one hundred million prayers asking for relief from trials and tribulations existing in the world, but why aren't our prayers being answered?

I have heard the Pope pray, the bishops, the evangelists, and their subordinates of differing denominations pray. Each year on Christmas, Easter, and Thanksgiving they pray for peace; likewise, I have gone to churches and listened to the preacher's sermon. Afterward there is always the request in prayer for peace and love, yet the conditions of peace never prevail nor has it been forthcoming. Yes, mankind wants peace and love, yet is it true the way to this divine situation can only come about if God grants it to us? I have attended the Million Man March and witnessed the Promise Keepers prayer event. Each of these events resulted in people praying for God to give us direction and salvation from the things that are torturing our daily lives This is what we are told to believe: God will, on the day of resurrection, save all those that believed in Him and His law

As you read, imagine, if you will, that God has come. You are prepared to walk through the gates of Heaven, aren't you? You went to the communities of those that are in poverty just yesterday, and gave to its inhabitants your love. When you looked down on that person or persons who were, in your considered opinion, sinners, you did so with the intent of lifting up your fellow man -or was it with contempt, frustration, or aggravation? Did you consider people who had less than you degradation of life, or as people who needs your intervention of kindness and love? The murderer locked in a prison cell-did you want for this person to redeem his horrible deed or did you decide for God that he was unworthy of redemption and salvation?

Take into consideration the many questions that will be asked of you on this day of resurrection. The law of love requires all humanity to act in deeds alone, not simply in prayers that are empty and insignificant. To recognize the Lord in prayer is not sufficient of itself to ensure your entrance into the gates of Heaven; it is the deeds and actions of mankind alone that serves the cause for God's divine intervention.

God will not act for us; we must act for ourselves. That is our responsibility to society, the universe, and to life.

We must compel ourselves to deal with saving our own planet and its inhabitants. God has revealed new answers to life so that we can do as we raise our children to do and that is to be responsible for our own actions and deeds. If we teach our children to honor and live by the codes of Gods love and to love each other, then we can expect the best results from them. If they choose to dishonor what has been taught them, then the worst consequences will prevail. No parent can stop the consequences for bad acts or deeds committed by their children; a parent, however, may try to change what has been done by providing restitution to those that have become the victims of their child's reckless deed or act. They must also help their children to rehabilitate and take responsibility for their act, in which case they must be treated through medical science and social practices to determine their problem. This must be done in order to help them not repeat the same offense.

It is in this vein that God has provided to mankind these Messages. We, His children, have committed acts that have lead us down the road of uncertainty and doom. Our ancestors, in their quest for a better understanding of truth, restructured the teaching of the prophets. Each succeeding generation of religious teachers has bent the truth to their own satisfaction and verification; consequently, humanity has lost sight of the true light. However, the Heavens have opened once again to shed light on the way toward our redemption and salvation: the way of love is the law of life. It is not the destruction and condemnation of man and His created world by God that will lead man into the gates of paradise. In fact, what Professor Robert Abrams taught me in relation to his creed is correct. I can only see the need for one correction, and that is: "God made each and all of us geniuses, the creation and carriers of great extraordinary creative life powers. He gave us the power, the means, the methods, the authority, and the responsibility to transform ourselves and the world for life's abundant growth and reproduction in creative freedom and peace in the here and now."

** Humanity has faced many hardships as a result of believing that God would perform a miracle and save the world from the clutches of evil.

** What is done in Heaven must be done on Earth by the human race. Paradise must come as a result of mankind's own intervention to correct his own mistakes.

** All religious institutions have served to instruct mankind on how to reach paradise, but until now the information has been mystical and mysterious.

** Although the messages are mystical, they have been institutionalized within the framework of human society. They have served to sooth and provide some peace of mind as to the question of what happens after death.

** This false sense of security has lead mankind to pray in abundance to God for help and relief from their troubled world.

** People are willing to go to Heaven, but are unable to practice the law of God on Earth.

** Mankind has been given the responsibility to protect the planet, and to cherish all living creatures on the earth, yet humanity cries out like children to God for help.

** God will not perform any miracles because it is against His will to make mankinds task an easy ordeal.

** He has given us the power, the means, the methods, and the authority to transform life into life-fulfilling ways.

** We as Gods children have grown into adults and now must be accountable and responsible for our own deeds and actions. Mankind with his own free will, can build paradise on Earth.

Early Answers

The Messages reveal something new. They now make it possible to relate to both understandings of mankind with respect to religion and science. Our ancestors have depicted for us images of God, and these images served to bring us into an awareness of God's existence. Do you think it is possible for you to realize that God is a spirit and did not create man in His physical image? Yet, these physical images have kept us in contact with Him, so it has been to the benefit of mankind that we look upon the face of God. We must, however, come to comprehend God as He really is. Upon doing so, only then can we realize that our commonality lies in our being like God, but without the mortal body. Humanity's challenge at this time is to come to the realization that we are spirits that have lived within our mortal bodies. Our bodies are different, but our spirits are the same.

To understand these revelations, one must search their conscience for truth. Unlike the Bible and other books of religion, this truth is not based on speculation, intuition, or magic. One has to consider that if God could create this entire universe simply by uttering "let there be," He would have made it possible for man to see His world from some different aspect, instead of just commanding man to believe in His word until His return to earth. In other words, it would appear that mankind would not have reached a point of confusion about life and creation. Mankind must now strive to reach a new ideal so as to bring religion into one unified context, and that can only be accomplished by coming to terms with one religion. It is at this time that we must see "Supplementology (The Almighty's religion For the Universe), as the essential element for obtaining just that: it is another chance to take stock of ourselves and heed that which we have only guessed.

Consider this: during the various stages of your life you won dered about God. You felt that He existed; however, you could not understand why He did not live up to your expectations. Many times you may have pondered the questions of who and what is God? Society has presented images of someone you could talk to about your troubles and problems. You could pray to God for all of your needs to be fulfilled, your only requirements was to believe in Him and obey His Commandments. As such, you had faith in knowing that He would somehow save the world from destruction. He would rescue the hungry, the unloved, the rejected, and the suffering people of the world. You prayed continuously for God's intervention on mankind's behalf. As the conditions of life prevailed in a disorderly fashion, you began to reconsider the power of God.

From the earliest of mankind's existence, the greatest tragedies of human existence always seem to prevail and yet the worlds conditions are somehow unchanged. Starvation, war, greed, and injustices raged on while we were told to reform and become obedient to God until He comes to save the world from suffering and sin. But when is He coming? Sunday is the day that Christians set aside to worship and show appreciation for Him, yet hungry people starve every day until death deals its crushing blow, lurching forth its victim to a sweet Heaven or horrible Hell.

We have seen ourselves involved in the proliferation of arms and nuclear weapons, often over issues of religion, yet God has not revealed His face. The grand illusion: does one ever see God, or is He like disappearing smoke, vanishing to an unknown dimension? Neither our naked eyes nor the use of the most powerful telescope can reveal where God is in the universe, but hunger is not an illusion, nor is destitution.

Humanity must realize that God wants the spirit to rise to a level where it can recognize that physical matter (bodies) and spirit must work cooperatively to create conditions on this planet that will ensure happiness. God cannot help, not because He is inca pable or uncaring, but because we must find our own way to resolve our created problems.

What is the answer? As you begin this path toward a different and new understanding of our world, take with you the implements of faith. Throw away your knapsack of conventions and traditional beliefs, or at least place them to the side of the road. In fact, dump out the contents of your upbringing and prepare to pick up new pieces of delight and wonderment.

The journey you are about to start will require that you open your spiritual eyes, listen with your knowledgeable ears, and feel within your heart a new sense of reality and belief. The implements of faith which are required for this journey are trust, desire, will, and belief.

Let's listen to the superior spirit Voltumato as he discussed the subject of mankind and the road we have allowed ourselves to follow with the Message Bearers:

Volturnato

(September 2, 1944)

"The human beings of the Earth are still very young, still influenced strongly by matter. Their ascent is endlessly difficult and sometimes tortuous. A simple observer might even feel that this road leads downward, not upward, but it may only seem that way. The Almighty has trusted human beings and their abilities to conquer matter and ljft it to the level of spirit, and sooner or later that will happen. In this work there are two might helpers-God and Satan.

"I am not seeking to place blame on human beings or to drive them to despair; rather to show to them their present state, and how they should not be. That is the only aim of my message.

"How, indeed, is the proud ruler of Earth at the present time, the human being? Let us open the eyes of our merciless mind and observe him.

"As I have already said, the human being is still very far from the ideal that the Almighty sees in him. The Almighty gave to the human being a free will, but the human being himself has not used this free will; he is not free. He is a miserable slave-the slave of humankind. The human being does not belong to himself. He not only is not able to do what he wants, but he has to do what he does not like to do. His laws ask him to serve mankind, the state, the country, and the family. It is impossible to think about an absolutely free human being, but we have the same difficulties in understanding his slavery.

"Through the laws of the state of humankind, and through the will of the ruler, an obligation is forced on human beings to live notfor themselves but to live for others. The human being does not need much bread for his food, nor much material for his clothing, nor a spacious castle in which to live. It should be easy for him to get everything he needs in an easy way, but it is not so. The human being has to work from early morning to late evening to be able to feed, clothe, and provide shelter for those who are not working. And there is an endless number of them: beggars, idlers, wealthy people, clergymen, clerks, rulers, and immense and completely unneeded armies.

"The social system of mankind is a system of slavery now, because the state of humankind was formed in the wrong way. There are wrong ideas and aims of human in the states of being. Every human being and every state is striving to be happy separately, by itself, alone. That is impossible: humankind is one great family. Can you tell me what radical differences there are among the nations? None! They could be happy members of one whole family.

"Brothers and sisters are quarrelsome. Every one of them thinking only about him/herself and his/her own wealth. Each is trying to get something from his/her siblings, causing obstruction of work and waste of time for themselves and others as well. Unnecessary quarrels and fighting make family life like hell. It robs it of success, prosperity, and happiness. Such a situation exists with mankind today. Human beings in the name of the state and the law are needlessly interfering in the personal lives and feelings of other human beings. They not only force others to do work that is not pleasant, but they even force others to love what is hated, thereby forcing them to hate the work that is loved.

"The human being uses everything to reach his! her imagined prosperity and wealth, where he! she hopes to find happiness. To reach this happiness, helshe uses all means: lies, cheating, deceit, pandering, slandering, stealing, and killing. He! she loses his honor, respect, and name- but helshe will not stop. There is nothing so sacred that it cannot be used to reach this aim.

"God sent to human beings His divine envoy, Christ, with teachings of love and happiness. Not being able to resist these teachings, human beings took them over and used them for their own purposes. The servants of the Church with the cross of Christ on their chests cursed the unbelievers. They took away their belongings and burned them at the stake. They created a distasteful and horrible idea of hell and, with the help of this idea, drew the people to a more nasty paradise. The clergymen not only were not ashamed to preach hate in the churches of God, but they even helped rulers drive people to wars and death. They not only helped, but even took swords into their own hands in the name of God. With prayers to an ever-merciful God on their lips they cut off the heads of the people.

"Now they use the teachings of Christ in order to gain prosperity and honor on Sundays. The job of a clergyman is better than other jobs. To serve God is so easy! Even thinking is not needed. Everything that is needed is obtainable in a thick gold book. And God, dear God, keeps silent and will not punish anyone, for helshe serves this God.

"But humankind, in spite of being blind, sees that something is wrong here. The name of God starts to disappear from the lips of the people and ever more frequently they use the word "devil". To them the devil is no more believable, but his teachings seem more practical.

"With love in their hearts, he and she meet at the altar and swear to be faithful to each other to the grave. Who needs these base lies? Everyone knows that there is no eternal love or eternal faithfulness. If some run crying the next day for a divorce, people are surprised and a discussion arises. If there is divorce after some months or years, that is a common thing. There is a corner of the world where marriage is changed into a sport. I would say it is veiled prostitution, which is still practiced in some countries.

"Count for me the number of faithful people in marriage. I am afraid that it will not require a long period of time or much work. In family life human beings take off their mask. That is the basis for the tragedy in a family, for marriages are contracted with masks. Very frequently in family life human beings show themselves to be worse than they actually are, for what they are not allowed to show to others they are able to show to their partner in marriage, or mistress. The law helps them to bind this partner to them. Very frequently his trouble on the job, his moodiness, and his failures gives vent to each other. They become scapegoats. Control of oneself in front of loved ones is not needed. To dress decently is not needed. One may walk around in a torn robe and with an unwashed face. One does not need to deal with one's shortcomings and physical defects. So love dies and Satan laughs, as the people say.

"Now Satan tells the people why these things happen this way. He is not laughing, but He is smiling bitterly.

"To envy one's friend, to kick them when they are down, to betray them, to seduce their spouse -these still are not sins, especially when he/she covers the face with the thick smoke of a friend ly cigarette. The human being uses everybody, including the most beautiful and noble words and ideas. Neither the governments nor rulers say that they actfor the sake of themselves. No-everything is done only for the sake of the nation. For the sake of the nation castles are built where the people somehow are not let in. For the sake of the people rocks are shaped and jails are built. For the sake of the people grain is sown that is sent to foreign countries for an exchange of gold. For the sake of the people wars are carried out. In these wars the people die, their homes are destroyed, and their work comes to naught. For the sake of the people, time is taken away from the nation; the same with happiness and freedom, and even life is taken away. But is the nation gaining something from it all? There are some gains, but not for the entire nationonly for a tiny group of people. The strangest thing is that the nation believes the words of the rulers and governments. Even these rulers and governments think that they act in favor of the nation and only through the benefits to the nation will they also benefit. The human being is not able to see all this. Money was created as a means of exchange, but now is looked on as a selfvalued thing. For money, a human being gives away everything, although the accumulated mountains of money are actually and completely useless to him/her.

"Humankind has lost the perception of correlation to reality. Humankind changes everything to meaningless ideas and words, including the most sacred feelings. Brotherhood, a friendship of weapons welded together with blood-are nice and noble words but they are only hollow words. The brothers of yesterday are enemies today. They fight and blame their friends and brothers of yesterday, and they kiss their enemies. The treaties and statements of faith have only the value of the paper on which they are written. Only profit and a more favorable situation are the decisive factors.

The noble, beautiful and appealing speeches that seem as if they are coming from the heart-how much is real'

Today maybe some thing, but tomorrow, under different circumstances-nothing! The heart of a human being is like an empty drum upon which the beating sticks of life's situation are falling. The emptier the heart, the stronger the drum sounds. Words, streams of words, rivers of words, lakes of words, seas of words, oceans of words pour over the unhappy human being. His/her weak sense of perception sinks in these floods of words. Words have lost their meaning; work has lost its appeal. Human beings still have not found an aim for their lives.

"I have to finish, for my high ruler is waiting for me. I repeat: madness has taken over mankind today. Millions are dying. Thousands of cities that were built by entire generations are wiped off the Earth, together with their immeasurable value. Who has given anyone the right to destroy the work of your ancestors and ruin the value created by them? The human being of today? Who gave you the right to put the unbearable load of renewal work on the shoulders of your future generations? Have you thought about how much it will cost humankind for your blind hate and madness? Do you recognize the responsibility you have put on your conscience, the lives of millions killed and crippled, and the unnecessary destruction of cities? If the insane would have escaped from the asylum, grabbed all power on earth into their hands, they would have done less damage to it than you-the chosen and wise! Now, with your mind overcome with despair, you are accumulating new and horrible weapons, and would like to envelop the Earth in deadly gas again.

"I asked the Almighty that this page of the most dreadful and villainous deeds in the history of humankind be closed, so that the other pages might not stay half empty, stained with sweat and tears." (Homics 1976, pp. 364368)

** Physical images of God have allowed mankind to visualize our Creator; however, mankind must now realize that we are exactly like Him in a spiritual sense.

** Our God is not a physical entity. He is purely spiritual and does not exist in the universe as a physical entity.

** Human being must begin to recognize that we are made in His likeness as spiritual entities residing in matter (flesh and blood).

** God wants mankind to rise to the level of understanding its spiritual entity and conquering matter.

** Mankind has been given a free will to choose its own course, to overcome matter, and rise to the level of the spirit.

** The human being is still young and very far from the ideals the Creator sees in him.

** The human being has not used his free will to overcome the influences of matter.

** The human being does not live for himself/herself but for others. He/she works for the good of those that choose not to work. This includes the beggars, idlers, wealthy people, clergymen, clerks, rulers, and immense and completely unneeded armies.

** Social systems dictate that people serve themselves and the state separately. Human beings are striving to be happy individually alone or as an individual country or state.

** It is impossible to be happy alone because mankind is one great family.

** Human beings use everything that is sacred to reach his/her imagined prosperity and wealth, where he/she hopes to find happiness.

** Religion was given a new meaning by those that espoused the truth of religion. Religious leaders of ancient times committed atrocious acts and deeds that resulted in people losing their lives and their property in the name of helping Christ to reform the unbelievers.

** The teachings of Christ are now used to gain prominence, recognition, and honor on Sundays.

** Human beings are lost and still searching for the meaning of their existence.

** Human beings must begin to understand that the consequences for its actions can result in dire devastation. Mankind must resolve to use their free will to overcome the needs of matter (accumulation of material wealth) and resort to identifying with its spiritual needs primarily.

CREATION

In as much as the human race evolved in different natural environments, we as human beings are very different, but it now must be understood and reconciled that this evolutionary process did not change the true origin of humankind. Neither was the creation of the universe a spontaneous act by God: the creation of the universe deals with something much greater than what we previously believed. All humankind came from the same source. Even though the human race has an outward physical characteristic that denotes some differences, these differences have come about as a result of different climatic environments. The human being that evolved in the equatorial regions of the planet have darker skin because their bodies needed more protection from the sun; on the other hand, those human being that had migrated further to the north had less need for protection from the sun and therefore their skins were lighter. It can be traced throughout the course of human evolution that human being migrated to different parts of the planet throughout the millions of years that it took mankind to reach the level we have thus far reached, so in the course of human evolution mankind has had to change physically according to the particular environment in which each "race" settled.

Before we take this opportunity to further understand the questions that have so long prevailed within the minds of men, let us examine the spiritual entities that will give us this new perspective on creation. You are about to hear from the Almighty's chief spirits Alpha and Omega. In the Bible, the Alpha and the Omega denote our beloved deity, God. The words themselves represent the beginning and the end; that God was the beginning and will remain so until the end of time. In other words, God is eternal.

At this time, however, you will be listening to spiritual entities that are named Alpha and Omega. How can that be, you may ask? I asked myself the same question when I first read the Messages. I knew nothing of these entities; as a matter of fact, I was taught that there was only one God and that He was the Alpha and the Omega. I also thought God was the Almighty. I was not aware that there existed another entity named the Almighty. I was confused to say the least. The Almighty, God, Alpha, and Omega, I discovered, were all different entities, each different as apples fallen from the branch of its tree. These entities were the same but were also different.

The Almighty is the creator of the universe, and spirits were created from His spirit. This means that the Almighty creates your spirit, as well as all spirits of the universe. Who then, you may ask, is the Almighty? An entity that can claim He created our loving God, as well as my very own spirit. I can only say what I have said throughout this information; you will learn something new and different as it relates to your life, the world, and the universe. How you react to it depends on your ability and spiritual capacity to accept this information. The contradictions about life and creation that have arisen as a result of man's growth and development can now be answered with much more conclusiveness. It can also be seen that this new revelation can serve to clarify and verify man's idea on how the world and the universe came into existence.

Alpha and Omega have been given the responsibility to reveal the true story of the universe's creation, and are speaking to mankind because the Creator of the universe has given them permission to reveal this story. They are chief spirits. What this title means is that they are so close to the entity of the Almighty that they can communicate with Him directly. None of the other spirits are directly connected with Him-the Almighty speaks through these two spirits alone. Even in this capacity these two spirits consider themselves to be as dust at His feet. Therefore, Alpha and Omega has authority throughout the entire universe. Their responsibilities and authority cover the whole realm of the Heavens. In listening to these spirits, you will discover as I did that what they express can be taken as reliable and true. Of course, there is room for doubt and questions concerning this aspect of truth, but you can only come to have faith that what is being revealed is true.

For every question that comes to mind about life and creation and the universe, these messages will explain, as they have for me, the real answers and truth. Since I will be discussing the subject of spirits and their functions in a later chapter, I will proceed to share with you how the universe came into existence, as heralded by the chief spirits of the Almighty, Alpha and Omega.

Alpha And Omega

(June 4, 1944)

"We are the superior spirits of the Almighty: I, Alpha, the ruler of the beginning, the past, and the future; I, Omega, the ruler of the future and of the death, and promulgator of the thoughts of the Almighty. We are speaking to you, the nations of the Earth, in the name of the Almighty.

"Once, in the vacuum of the universe, there was only the immaterial spirit of the Almighty. The Almighty and matter-a motionless and dense fog filled endless space. Motionless matter with inert energy filled the universe. An overwhelming peacefulness and intolerable silence ruled the world. This peacefulness and silence had no beginning and no end. This peacefulness had no direction and no plan. It was hostile and unbearable to the living spirit of the Almighty. Unthinkably lonely was the spirit of the Almighty in this inert world of matter. To live in this motionless and aimless world was intolerable to the immortal spirit of the Almighty.

"Despondent, the Almighty in a fit of impatience smashed the world of matter. A cosmic storm broke out. The matter surged and moved. The sleeping energy in the matter became loose, and in the space of the world a whirlwind of matter started to spin. Matter started to change. Once started, the matter was unable to stop or calm down. Fields of mist arose. They condensed more and more, and your so-called suns were created. They hurtled through space at tremendous speeds. They collided with each other, creating gigantic fires in the universe. They separated in the space of the universe, but behind them new small stars and suns were left, which cooled off and became dense and dark. In that way the planets were created.

"The Almighty conformed the matter to His laws and started to investigate and mold this world. As helpers to Him, and in order not to be alone, He created spirits from His spirit, but He did not reach His second goal. He still remained lonely, because His created spirits were the same as Himself, only divided into many fractions. Imagine, if you can, that you are able to divide yourself into many fractions-would that save you from loneliness? Every part of you would think, talk, and do what you would do. You would see yourself uncountable times multiplied in the mirror of a broken surface. To be able to save yourself and find friends, you would have to go a different way-you would have to bear children.

"On many planets circumstances caused the matter to solid into rock and earth. Over the Earth clouds floated, rain came down, rivers rippled, waterfalls roared, the sea rose in waves, and the wind wailed. It seemed that the matter was living, but that was only in one's imagination. And the spirits asked the Almighty: You asked us to rule over the stars and planets, but this ruling has no aim and no order. For instance, why is rain falling on the Earth, which is without life and empty? Why are rivers streaming to seas that are empty and meaningless?' And the Almighty again felt alone and disheartened.

"Yes, the vastness of the universe was glittering with stars; yes, on the planet there was noise and movement, but everything was the same: matter without life. It was hostile and unbearable, this inert matter.

"Time passed, and then the Almighty started a confrontation with the entity of matter. He decided to create live matter. After a long, seemingly endless fight, the great moment came when matter came alive. Atoms created the first molecule and the dead matter started to live and breathe. Live beings cropped up. The Earth was covered with grass and trees. The water, the surface of the Earth, and even the air was filled with insects, animals, fish, and birds.

"Now the Almighty and the spirits were standing ready for a new task: to develop that living matter in such a way it would be able to reach an ideal fullness, and would be able to understand the spirit and rise to the level of the spirit. And in understanding the spirit its hostility would cease, so that matter and spirit would be merged to reach the highest aim-the creation of the most ideal world.

"But there was one more aim-the wish of the Almighty not to be alone. To have spirits that would be able to understand Him and help Him develop the world was His aim, but His aim still was not reached. The Almighty started His second work of stupendous creation. He had given brain to the animals, i.e., a complicated center of nerves, because the animals had to move and look for food. They also had to fight and adapt themselves to the demands of life and nature. This center of nerves, which up to now had been led by instinct, He spiritualized with His spirit: He created mankind on Earth and other creatures on some of the planets, but not many. For humankind He developed a wonderful brain, and gave this wonderful laboratory to the spirit.

"With that, the circle of loneliness was closed. The spirits of the Almighty, reincarnating in the bodies of human beings, are fighting with the hostile matter. The fight is not one of destruction, but a fight of resurrection and transformation. The spirits give much to the matter and they also get much from the matter, resulting in changes in themselves. In that way they help the Almighty to develop the ideal world and conquer the inertia of matter - not to hate the Almighty's spirit that forced it (matter) to live and move. The duty of a human being is-by combining the strength of spirit and matter-to rise above the existing laws of nature and create an ideal, complete, and immortal being who will rise to the level of divinity, and together with the Almighty take over the further development and ruling of the universe. That is the aim and sense of a human's life.

"Temporarily, until matter is transformed and an immortal body is created, the spirits have to travel from one body into another. The aim of humankind might still seem to you to be great and unreachable, but it only seems that way because human beings are led by the immortal spirit of the Almighty.

"With this the Almighty has reached His second aim. He, the Father, with the help of matter, created a son for Himself-a human being that will be He and also not He.

"Remember only one thing, that now you are able to understand the Almighty and His created world. You can understand the sense behind creation and also the idea and aim of life. Understanding all of that, you yourself have to understand what you have to do to reach this aim. For those who do not like to fol- low the call of the Almighty, He leaves only one other way- the way to nothingness (non-existence). To those who are not willing to follow the call of the Almighty to develop the world and reach the height of the spirits, the Almighty is neither promising them paradise, nor scaring them with hell: He simply allows them to be unneeded dust thatflows through the space of the universe into the darkness of nothingness (non-existence).

"The Almighty divided Himself into two high spirits: God and Satan, who are visible to the spirits and whom they can reach. God has the right to raise the spirit of living things and human beings, and to treat them with rays of love. He has the right to listen to human beings and help them. Satan has the right to test human beings, to punish, and to destroy them. Looking from the human being's point of view, God has all the good and Satan has all the evil; therefore pray only to God, because the Almighty will not listen to you. Pray to God not with words, but with good deeds.

"We, the superior spirits of the Almighty - Alpha and Omega-bring to you ten (the original Message Bearers) and all human beings the blessing of the Almighty and the love of God!"

"Be bright as the sun and strong as steel.." (Homics 1976, pp. 190-193) (Mezins 1992, pp. 49-52)

It is important to remember at this point what was mentioned relating to spiritual entities: we are all created from the Almighty's spirit; thus, all spirits are different with regard to their specific abilities, functions, and duties. God and Satan's duties will be discussed in detail in a later chapter. We must, however, for the first time realizes since man's creation who God and Satan are, and what their true functions entail. At this point, however, let us concentrate on the truth of life and creation, and the aim of the human being.

Truth About Creation

THE CLERGY, ALONG WITH SCIENTISTS, MAY now approach the philosophy of the "big bang" theory not as a possibility but as reality. This quote from Messages to Mankind, "Despondent, the Almighty, in a fit of impatience, smashed the world of matter" lends considerable support and credibility to the ideas man has discovered concerning the creation of the universe. Let us look at what the Big Bang theory means in relation to man's discovery. In 1917, William deSitter put forward the idea that the whole universe might be expanding or contracting. Then in 1927, George Lemaitre proposed the Big Bang theory: the universe was born in a cataclysm when a dense ball of material erupted. According to Lemaitre's theory, space and time began on "a day without a yesterday," when all the raw material for today's universe exploded from a point of infinite density. In 1929, Edwin Hubble showed that faint nebulae were receding from Earth at great speeds, supporting the idea of an expanding universe. Recently in 1992, George Smoot, a physicist from the Lawrence Berkeley Laboratory, discovered the "missing link" that could prove the Big Bang theory. As reported by the Washington Post on May 3, 1992, Dr. Smoot's discovery uncovered a missing link to the theory of how the universe came into existence. His team found "ripples in the fabric of space time." They believe that these ripples were "in the first trillionth of a second of the explosive moment of creation, dictating the shape and form of today's universe, including its island of inquisitive humanity."

In the Bible Genesis L• 2 reveals how the world came into existence: "And God said, let there be light and there was light." Our scientists do not dispute what God revealed to man; they only provide a basis for understanding what our ancestors could not comprehend. Adam Ford talks about the creation of the universe in his book entitled "Spaceship Earth." He states: "For about a million years the universe was an expanding fireball of light. When it grew cooler, the first atoms formed. Then gravity took over. It pulled together the small atomic particles within the great ball of gas and light. The material of the universe separated into billions of enormous clouds and, within these clouds, the stars were born." Thus, the Bible revealed to man of that time only that which he could perceive with regard to his limited knowledge of the universe and life.

The formation and transformation of the Universe can be understood in more detail today because of man's increased ability to investigate his world. This new "revelation" provides man an opportunity to explore without bias concerning religion and science of our universe. Our ancestors were told the truth, but only within their capacity to comprehend life, as they knew it. Our scientists, cosmologists, astronomers, and physicists will learn more of our universe and its creation; it now, however, can be understood and corroborated with religion.

In Genesis, chapter two, verse seven, it states: "and the Lord God formed man of the dust of the ground, and breathed into his nostrils the breath of life; and man became a living soul." Again we see that our ancestors were told about the creation of man in a simplified form. Due to man's inability to understand the true nature of life and creation, God revealed some sense of the creation of life. We must look, however, at what has now been revealed to and discovered by man. In our schools we are taught that man was first an animal and evolved into his present form after many years.

Man has always sought an explanation of his doubts and questions concerning life, and he has learned something about the mysteries imposed upon him, but let us put into perspective how he has learned or discovered the answers to his questions. First, this segment of the Messages reveals that man has what animals do not have: the creative spirit of the Almighty. Man thinks that he has a far more complicated and superior brain than the animals, but let us look at early man and try to understand why his development was different from that of animals. Why did man seek an identity and understanding of his world?

As mentioned earlier, the same molecules and atoms that make up the brain of animals are the same in humans. Scientists have assumed that humans are a higher animal form, and conclude that the human brain's thinking ability alone controls the development of our societies and world.

Therefore, since animals have been unable to defeat or control mankind, it leaves to reason that they are not capable of out thinking human beings. Science has uncovered certain ideas relating to this understanding, such as the evolution of man's brain and body. Mankind's brain has increased in size, as has his physical dimensions. Scientists have shown the gradual changes that have taken place in our bodies and brain over the past 14 million years.

The Readers Digest's The Last Two Million Years illustrates this point: "As man's brain became bigger, responding to the demands of more complex hunting, he became taller, with more refined teeth and jaws. As man's hands became capable of more precise manipulation, the implements he made became more sophisticated. By two million years ago tools were being made to a set pattern; and by the time of Homo Sapiens tools were finished to a higher standard than function required." (pp. 13)

Man And Animals

Now let us look at other animals that have grown up with man, such as horses, birds, fish, dogs, and cattle. These animals are also not quite like their predecessors of prehistoric times; their bodies have changed and they have adjusted to anew environment, just as humans have.

But look at the differences between the two groups: you are reading this book and comprehending the content of it, but could our ancestors of the prehistoric period begin to understand any portion of this material? Imagine you were given the power to transport a prehistoric man into the present. Would you feel that this person could function or would be capable of learning to read, write, or spell? Even under the best conditions of isolated laboratories and given the genius of our day to teach them about science and current social standards it would be impossible.

Man, since his creation, has had a number of situations not unlike animals. He has had to fend for himself, both for and against the environmental elements of his world. He also lived in caves and tree trunks, killed for his food, invaded other men's homes, and produced food for himself. Why then is he still not like the bird, lion, rodent, and the bee? How is it that he can change his environment and the animals cannot? We both have existed since creation.

Both the cat and dog have been domesticated, for they were around when man was a beast himself, and yet neither has the power of logic, deduction, and the ability to comprehend more than the instincts with which they were born; they only have the power of inertia. Perhaps it can be deduced that God gave dominance to man over the animals, but how and why was this done?

It is believed that God created man in His own likeness, thereby enabling man to have greater intelligence than animals. If this is true, then which of His nations is more in His likeness? Are the other nations not in His likeness in the same situation as the animals? Allowing that nations of men vary in their likeness, then it should be reasoned that only one nation is of His likeness. As we can see, however, this is poor deduction and logic.

Is it right therefore to conclude that animals live by instinct alone, while man lives by instinct and spiritual ability? This spiritual ability is part of the Creator's spirit, which is incarnated into the human body. We will learn more of what the spirit is and what it can do in a later chapter. Lets take a look at what science has to offer in the sense of what has been uncovered relating to the evolution of animals. Richard Carrington, a Scientific Fellow of the Zoological Society of London, states: "Little more than a century ago, few people realized that the diverse array of mammals were not only related to one another but to all other living things. Religion taught that each individual type of animal had been created by God to fulfill a special role in the world. The idea that the mighty elephant, the tiny shrew, the lithe and graceful panther, the monkey, apes and even man were in a very real sense cousins would have been regarded at best as a mad delusion and at worst blasphemy. Yet we know beyond a doubt that these creatures can trace their ancestry back to a common stock.

"The revelation of this fact is, of course, due to the discovery of the principle of organic evolution. The idea of the evolution of all life was discussed by ancient Greeks, but after them it was forgotten for more than 2,000 years and men's minds were preoccupied with more magical interpretation of nature. It was not until the middle of the 18th Century that the idea was reborn, this time with new vitality. A century later in 1859, Charles Darwin's On the Origin of Species by Means of Natural Selection was published. This classic book presented the story of evolution so clearly that it could no longer be rationally denied, and later works have served to confirm its basic truth.

"Very briefly, the theory of evolution comprises the idea that all living things belong to one great family and that later more complex forms have developed from simpler forms that preceded them. The various members of this family became differentiated over many millions of years by the process known as 'natural selection' This process can operate because individual organisms from time to time produce definite heritable variations, known as

'mutations,' in the germ cells that give rise to next generations. Thus, in any given environment, there will be individuals who, through favorable mutation, have become better adapted to their way of life than their fellows. These individuals will be more likely to remain alive and reproduce themselves, and nature can therefore be said to have 'selected' that type for survival from among its less well-equipped rivals. This process is repeated in each generation, with different qualities selected in different environments. Thus, different' species' are eventually established, each with its own adaptations to its particular circumstances.

"According to findings of the latest research the history of the earth is at least 4.5 billions years. No more than half of this immense span of time, however, has been characterized by the evolution of living organisms. Through chemical reactions on the shores of early rivers or seas, the first tiny one-celled organisms known as 'protozoans' probably developed. As the generations passed, life increased in variety and complexity, and higher and higher kinds of organisms evolved. First there were soft-bodied creatures such as sponges and jellyfish, then creatures with protective shells. After these came a sequence of backed boned animals, or ' vertebrates' represented in ascending order by fishes, amphibians, reptiles, and finally mammals and birds." (Carrington 1963, pp. 35-36)

All of this represents man's empirical data as it relates to discoveries dealing with the history of evolution. In contrast to this the Messages reveal why living organisms have evolved. We have been given the opportunity to hear the story of creation. But what happened after the Almighty created this universe?

A superior spirit of God, the spirit Santorino, will provide some additional information regarding the Almighty's task of creating living creatures from inert matter. Santorino's authority derives from God and He has been given the responsibility to assist God in helping to bring up humankind on planet earth.

Santorino

(December 5, 1954)

"Even though the process of creating the world has been examined already, let us return to it once more. In His loneliness, the Almighty thought for a long time as to how to escape this loneliness, and how to acquire spirits, who would not be He, Himself, in plural. He observed the lifeless, immobile matter, and pondered what to do. It was easy to create spirits, but that did not give Him anything. What will the spirits do in this lifeless space? Create living beings? What will they do in it and how will they be able to exist in it?

"So that living beings could exist, such conditions of life had to be first created in which they could exist and progress. Hence, the world had to be created first, or, more correctly, worlds. Matter had to be brought to life.

First, it had to be set in motion, and it was easy to do that, but that accomplished nothing. Laws had to be initiated to explain how this matter was to form, how it was to become the suns and planets, and how life could be sustained on these planets.

"Nowhere did He have models to mimic. He had to invent, think of, and create everything. Neither had He completed schools in which, mathematics, geometry, physics, chemistry, and all that is being taught, which give man the opportunity of creating and progressing. He had only mind, power, and will. From these three things, He created the world as you know it, and as you criticize it. Obviously, man can claim that his mind, too, can create much; that he can create the world in which he now lives-the skyscrapers, ships, airplanes, etc. All that, however, has been created slowly and gradually over many generations. You acquire this knowledge from your ancestors, acquire it in schools, and acquire it from role models. The Almighty lacked all of that. Therefore, He was simultaneously a teacher and pupil to Himself. This means that He learned how to create from His mistakes.

"As I have already said, He devised the laws for the formation of matter, for the creation of suns and planets, for their existence, and for the creation of living beings on the planets. You catch a butterfly and admire its beauty. You encounter an elephant and admire its stature and strength. You claim that God has created all that. Yes, indeed, the Almighty has created all that. That does not mean, however, that the Almighty directly created this beautiful butterfly, and this great and powerful elephant. Rather, He acts simpler, more practical and more genial.

"He created such conditions for life that living beings can come into existence, and, gave laws according to which they are to come into existence and form. Everything in the world transforms. Nothing living remains in the same place, and this living transforms the lifeless as well." (Mezins 1992, pp. 184-186)

You can see now that the Almighty did not create every being, and that He had to experiment with the elements of the universe to create conditions for matter to live. He did not know the exact chemistry that was needed for living beings to exist and survive. There were no models for Him to duplicate. Matter did not create life for itself; therefore, the

Almighty had to investigate and find ways for matter to live. The Almighty created many planets with many conditions in order to discover the right ingredients necessary for matter to live.

In His created world there existed only spirits created from His spirit. In His desire, however, to raise matter to a level of understanding the spirit world He had to create beings that would be able to sustain the living spirit. Initially, the matter was given a brain with the instincts to live and survive; later, He gave to a species of animal a part of His creative spirit. This animal, which later came to be known as human, has grown as a result of the spirit incarnating into matter or human bodies.

** The Almighty was alone in space. Matter existed but it was inert; matter and energy had no purpose or objective.

** The Almighty, in a fit of impatience, smashed the world of matter and made it move. This can be considered the point where the Big Bang took place.

** In order not to be alone the Almighty created spirits from His spirit, but that did not help the Almighty from being alone. These spirits were the same as He.

** The Creator then brought about a change in His method of producing spirits: He created new spirits or children from Himself.

** The Almighty created suns and planets from the matter, but they still had no purpose or goal. The matter remained dead.

** After a while the Creator decided to create live matter. The moment came when matter began to live. The atoms created the first molecules, and dead matter began to live and breathe.

** The Almighty and His spirits were faced with a new task: to form this matter to reach a level of perfection; to form this matter so that it could reach the level of understanding and comprehending the spirit.

** The Almighty had given the animals a brain with which to function for the purpose of survival and adapt to the demands of life through the use of instinct.

** He created man on our planet and He spitualized man's brain with His creative spirit.

** The spirits give to matter; as well, matter gives to the spirits the capability of transforming each other to a degree of approaching the Almighty's demands. That demand is to help create an ideal and immortal body and assist the Almighty in the further formation and ruling of the universe.

THE ROLE AND TASLZS OF SPIRIT AND MATTER

(Spirit & Body)

"WE HAVE LEARNED THUS FAR THAT the Almighty created the brain within animals in order for them to maintain and survive their environment, but we must look at why man was able to overcome his environment and become the master of his world. Why has man gained dominance over this world? It has been revealed that the Almighty gave to man His creative spirit. With this spirit of the Almighty we are able to utilize our brain to think and reason, allowing us to create, evaluate, explore, and discover ways by which we can assume the powers to change and create the ideal world. For the first time in human history man must come to understand that the creative spirit of the Almighty resides in man.

The Almighty wanted to create in matter a way to understand and cooperate with the spirit, so He gave to matter His spirit to help lift it to the degree of comprehending the spirit world. Through understanding the spirit, it would come to cooperate with the spirit and help the Almighty in the further formation, development, and ruling of the universe. As revealed by the chief spirit Santorino (June 8, 1944),

"Mans task is, with the aid of the wonderful laboratory, the brain, given to him to help the Almighty in this gigantic labor, while man is simultaneously raising himself and matter with the spirit, to the heights of immortality and perfection', next to the Almighty." (Homics 1976, pp. 200)

Man has taken steps to escape from the confines of this planet, and we are now able to explore the universe with our limited capabilities, but must we do so in the fashion of our ancestors? We explored this world to find out the fastest trade route to the Far East and to confirm the geometric shape of the Earth. We must come to terms with the fact that mankind can neither conquer nor control what is in fact not the possession of humanity. The aim and sense of creation has to be understood now. Perhaps you ask yourself has mankind reached a point where he can understand this new aspect of life? Has man grown sufficiently to comprehend that his being is not due to some great natural phenomenon, or simply because God created creatures to obey rules that will lead him to heaven? It would appear that the answer is yes. If our Creator had deemed it not possible, then certainly the Earth and all of its inhabitants would be subject to destruction or non-existence.

I believe an understanding of what "non-existence" means should be expressed at this point so as not to confuse it with the notion of "hell." Santorino explains this concept as follows:

Santorino

(June 8, 1944)

"Now I will speak more about nonexistence, which you some how cannot understand.

"The quantity of spirit and matter that fills the universe is unchanging. Nothing can be added and nothing can disappear completely; it can only be changed.

"The spirit of the Almighty is one, and He can be only divided; He is also divided into spirits. The spirit obtains individuality for a certain period of time or forever. The spirits who have justified the hopes of the Almighty obtain eternal individuality, but the rest lose it, flowing back to the spirit of the Almighty. This is called the nonexistence of the individual spirit. I will try to explain it to you with an example that might give you a remote idea.

"Let's assume that the water would be the spirit of the Almighty. With the blessing of the Almighty or the warmth of the sun the water is changed into vapor. The steam is condensed and it becomes water again, but in the form of individual drops of water. Now this drop of water lives separately from the mass of water, so it falls to the ground. It hits a leaf of a tree and is shining as a jewel in the rays of the sun, or it is drawn up by a tree or a flower. For the time being this drop of water becomes part of a plant, or even part of an animal. The other drops of waterfall into rivers, into lakes, or into the sea, and they flow together with the mass of water. They do not disappear, but they no longer exist in the same composition. The same thing happens to the spirits that are not able to become individuals. They all go to nonexistence and flow into the ocean of the spirits of the Almighty." (Homics 1976, pp. 201) (Mezins 1992, pp. 55-56)

In the course of studying these Messages, I was able to discover that there were many more spirits who ruled certain aspects of this world, some of whom I never before knew. I certainly questioned the truth of this revelation, but as I continued to grasp the understanding of these Messages, I could see myself as identifying with not only the truth but also with life in its fullest meaning. I could no longer identify with just being a human being-feeling my flesh but not my soul was impossibility. In coming to understand my soul, I also felt the realness of those who spoke to the Message Bearers.

While coming to terms with this new information about the creation of our spirits, other concepts prevailed. New spirits do not come with an automatic knowledge about their existence. New spirits must grow and develop in a place called the Lunar Fields, and after some passage of time the spirit can elevate and ascend to the Solar Fields. You are probably wondering about such a thing as these designations. In researching ancient civilizations, archaeologists have discovered that different cultures worshipped conceived gods and spiritual deities. These cultures represent the fact that earliest man had some concept of higher beings that were neither visible nor reachable to them. These beliefs ultimately lead mankind to some concrete distinctions and descriptions concerning our God of today.

In most instances, current civilizations and cultures adhere to the principle of one God, yet we do not lend any support to the thought of our ancestor's belief about the ascension of spirits to a higher degree. Many ancient civilizations recognized several different gods. Greeks and Romans had several gods they worshipped. Each nation and continent of people had some mystifying aspect concerning a supreme entity or being. Throughout the ages of man's transformation, it has been revealed that we acknowledged some form of afterlife. The Egyptians sent their dead pharaohs into the hereafter with the knowledge of traveling to another plane or level of life. Our current civilization teaches us to believe that our ancestor's beliefs had little or no basis for truth. As you will come to understand, there was a reason for why and how they came to believe what they did.

These new Messages have revealed to mankind the truth about the growth and development of our spirits. These Messages have a direct correlation to what our ancestors believed about the gods and the progress of the spirit. I would like to take you now to what has been revealed about the journey of our spirits from its inception through its process of growth and development. This brief explanation is not the total description of how the spirit develops; it is only a slight version of what the spirit can do while in the process of spiritual life. This information entails the formation of the spirit's eternal individuality. Listen to what the superior spirit Santorino has to say about the life cycle of our spirits:

Santorino

(April 9, 1944)

"I will speak about the Sun Planes now, but first a few words about the Moon Planes.

"The Moon Planes are under the control of Satan. Satan is not an evil spirit from the point of view of the Almighty. He is the one who has to test the spiritual abilities of the creations of the Almighty. By testing and punishing those, He has to bring them up.

"The souls or spirits who are in the Moon Planes can be compared to the soft material of pottery; that is, malleable and adjustable by a simple touch of the hand.

"In the Sun Planes there are spirits similar to earthenware that has already hardened, but they must be baked and painted. With clay that is soft, the potter acts without mercy. The pots that do not come out right are smashed and new ones are formed instead. The hard vessel is more difficult, as it is not so easily adjusted. The more complete the vessel is, the more valuable it is, and the vessel that is painted by an artist with his hands might be very expensive and valuable. Nobody wants to destroy it.

"In the Sun Planes there also is a school for spirits and a place for rest. They learn much from each other and from the high spirits. The higher they climb the higher they become, and more is bestowed on them.

"In the Planes of the Sun there are charming gardens. The melody of the rays of the Almighty is heard. The spirits have the choice of visiting all of the corners of the universe. They may ask to become guardian spirits of human beings. All the time they see the Temple of Deoss and the high spirits that emanate to and from it.

`By reincarnation the spirits grow and develop, or fall. Those who are not able to grow to the level of divinity or reject it, stay in the thirteenth circle, the so-called Island of Bliss. Here, there is everything that the spirit might want. He/she might also visit the Temple of Deoss. He/she might be a guardian spirit. He/she might also be reincarnated alone, or together with a lovely spirit in being on the planet of the blissful ones. They might also be reincarnated on other planets into bodies of so-called happy beings and enjoy all human beings.

"For the time being, nothing more can be said about the Sun Planes.

"You have already been told about the spirits who are on the way to the level of divinity or Almightiness.

"With this we have finished the discussion of this question." (Homics 1976, pp. 99) (Mezins 1992, pp. 32-33)

The analogy given here by the superior spirit Santorino may shed some light on the subject of how a spirit grows and progresses: it is with influence and corroboration with other spirits that we grow as individual spirits, as well as the process of incarnation of the spirit in the body.

The Lunar Planes is the beginning place for all spirits to begin the process of development. It is from the inception and creation of a newborn spirit that the process begins. It has been revealed through these Messages that a new spirit must begin to travel or ascend to the thirteen levels of the

Lunar Planes and at the same time it can be incarnated in a human body. After the completion of ascending through the various levels, the spirit then ascends to the level of the Solar Planes. At this stage it can become a guardian spirit for humans.

Here again the spirit must continue the process of growth and development. However, now the spirit inherits a new task and assignment: the spirit must try and reach the level of divinity. A spirit has to ascend through twelve levels of the Solar Field to reach this goal. The spirit is no longer alone with himself in this quest. The spirit must now take on the task of bringing matter (body) to the level of understanding the spirit world. The spirit is reincarnated in the body for generation after generation, and in the process Satan, who determines our spiritual abilities through our free will to commit good or evil deeds, tests spirits repeatedly.

The continued existence of a spirit is determined by its ability to progress toward understanding and comprehending the spirit world while incarnated in a human body. What this means is that the human must come to recognize its immortal spirit as a true entity. The body (matter) is mortal yet with the help of the spirit it can become immortal as well. This is the level of divinity that the spirit must ascend to. The capability of recognizing it immortality allows the spirit to reconsider the needs of its mortal body. In order to acquire eternal individuality, a spirit has to understand and comprehend the spirit world while being incarnated in the human body. This process amounts to helping the body (matter) to reach the level of the spirit as well.

So from its inception to the level of divinity the spirit is fulfilling the desire and will of the Almighty, and it is through this process of progression that we as spirits are following the will of God. However, let us look at how the spirits differ, as related to us by the high spirit Aksanto:

AKSANTO

(August 8, 1944)

"THE SPIRITS ARE DISTINCT. THERE ARE spirits who are completely inert in relation to other spirits. There are spirits who only observe the activity of living being. There are spirits who lead the spiritual activities of living beings. There are spirits who are able to materialize; that is, they can enable others to see them in their desired appearance as, for instance, Mortifero. There are not many of those spirits and their power is unlimited. There are also spirits who lead the destinies of worlds and help the Almighty in the work of creation and guidance. There are also superior spirits who are so close to the Almighty in their entity that they might be looked at as different faces of the Almighty." (Homics 1976, pp. 319)

We have been shown various aspects of the spirits. To come to a total understanding of what a spirit is, we must realize that we can no longer think of ourselves in terms of just brains and bodies. We must think in terms of our bodies and spirits. We cannot think of ourselves as a singular entity in nature and creation, but as a dual entity. The spirit, as revealed by these Messages, has been shown to be a definitive and distinctive entity. Out of the body the spirit is independent and can function on its own. The Almighty can only sanction its creation. We as body and spirit (human beings) can now approach life from a definitive aspect of what we actually are.

Because of two differing concepts pertaining to science and religion we have become lost in a void with regard to how mankind came to exist in our present state. Did God come to create the beautiful creatures we are today, or did we come to be what we are through evolution and nature?

These new Messages reveal a new assumption for mankind to consider. I will show what has been revealed about the evolution of spirits, as discussed by the superior spirit Santorino:

Santorino

(December 16, 1966)

"Concerning the spirits of the living beings, or souls, as they are called. The Almighty gave His spirit to Adam and Eve. They were the first people, as related in the Holy Scriptures. Let's not argue with your Holy Scriptures. Because of their simplicity, they are useful to us in the carrying out of our intentions.

"Sons and daughters were born to Adam and Eve. Adam's spirit divided himself into sons, and Eve's spirit into daughters. After Adam's death, his spirit returned to Heaven, and so did Eve's spirit, yet the parts of their spirits that had split off continued to live on Earth and divide again. Thus, the spirit of Adam and Eve still live within you, and they live in all people, but they are no longer entirely the spirits of Adam and Eve. They have transformed over time, just as living matter transforms.

"As you can see, by living together with the bodies for hun dreds of thousands of years, the current spirits have become entirely different spirits than the spirits of Adam and Eve. Since the spirit passes from the father's body into the son's body, and the mother's spirit into the daughter's body, the same spirit continues to live together with the bodies, which also transform under the uninterrupted guidance of the very same spirit. What then take place? The spirit of Adam's son after leaving his body, meets in Heaven with the spirit of Adam, the father. Two of Adams spirits meet each other, but while being one and the same, they are somewhat different already. They receive new tasks which depend on the abilities they have demonstrated during the time of incarnation on Earth." (Mezins 1992, pp. 354-355)

What this revelation shows, then, is that our spirits have evolved along with our bodies, that the fast process of evolution came as a result of the spirit being incarnated into a species of animal. This species of animal was not the familiar human that resides on our planet today; in fact, this revelation asserts that both the spirit and body have evolved simultaneously. I believe that man's definition of spirituality does not entail the aspects of eternity, purpose, and the reason for the existence of human beings. Religious leaders ask mankind to do good in order to reach a state of harmony with God, thereby providing man with a chance to be rewarded with eternal life upon or after death, but for what reason? Scientists understand the logic of infinity or eternity and perhaps see the body and brain as the perpetuation of human existence. But can human beings' lives be perpetual or eternally based on the brain and its functions alone?

** The spirit is a manifestation of the Almighty's spirit, and its purpose is to help matter reach the level of understanding the spirit world.

** By reaching the level of the spirit world, matter can then begin to reach a level of perfection and divinity. Matter and spirit can work cooperatively together to help in the further formation and ruling of the universe with the Creator.

** The spirit has to help matter to realize it potential to become as immortal as itself.

** The spirit has to incarnate in bodies until it has ascended to the level of divinity.

** The spirit has to ascend through two different Planes: the Lunar Planes and the Solar Planes.

** The Lunar Planes has thirteen levels and new spirits have to ascend through all of the levels and then they can receive an assignment to be incarnated into a human body.

** The Sun Plane has thirteen levels and spirits have to ascend through twelve of the levels. In the thirteenth circle they can choose to remain as eternal individuals or proceed forward to obtain the level of divinity.

** All spirits are independent and are assigned various tasks in accordance with their own specific abilities.

** The spirits have evolved along with human beings and they have existed since the creation of Adam and Eve. They were the first spirits on our planet to complete the Lunar Planes. When they reached that point they began to ascend through the thirteen levels of the Sun Planes and were assigned to bodies on our planet. The spirits of Adam and Eve and all spirits on our planet are descendants of them.

** Most spirits have been in existence for generations, which has resulted in spirits becoming different from their predecessors. Just as humans have evolved into different beings, so too have our spirits become different from our ancestral spirits.

Spirit, Matter, And Emotion

It has been revealed that matter alone is inert; that once matter is set into motion it cannot stop. Matter did not create life for itself. Observe a rock and you will notice the properties of this rock. It is simply an object: it does not hear, see, or feel. A rock is made up of the same substances that make up the body. All matter is comprised of the same substances, protons, neutrons, and electrons. These substances adhere to the same principles or laws regarding the structure of its existence. A molecule is a combination of two or more atoms the same kind or different. Molecules are held together by valence electrons. None of these substances have been shown to have any thinking capabilities.

Now let us look at a human being. You are reading this material and achieving this feat with your brain. Indeed, your brain is gray matter within your skull. But isn't the brain comprised of the same basic substance as the pitiful rock? Atoms, which are comprised of the protons, neutrons, and free electrons? Ask one of these three substances to recite back to you what you have just read. Ask them what you will decide to do later today or tomorrow. I am certain that this request can be viewed as foolishness. The point I am trying to make is that there is something greater directing you to read or think of future possibilities. It is not just the brain that allows you to deal with the circumstances of life.

In the beginning of man's evolutionary process all he had was his instincts. The animals of today still live by instinct alone. A dog has to wait for its master to feed him. The caretakers must attend to the animals in the zoo in order to survive. Animals in the wild survive by utilizing their natural inborn instincts to live. So the question becomes: why are human beings capable of learning and using what they learn to change their environment and the world, while the animal with its brain can only fend for itself, in terms of its own particular survival? What is the significant difference between humans and animals? They both have brains comprised of the same substances. All primates have some very similar traits and characteristics as human beings. Yet the gorilla, chimpanzee, and gibbon still have not reached the intellectual level of human beings. We both have been in existence for the same amount of time. Even though we have co-existed for millions of years, the human has gone on to dominate the world, and the primate is viewed as a spectacle at the zoo.

Something happened in a Brookfield, Illinois zoo, however, that caused the population to take note. A young child fell into a gorilla pit while he was visiting the zoo. The little boy was knocked unconscious. A female gorilla rescued the child and placed him out of harm's way so that the keepers could retrieve him. Was this an act of intelligence, or was it an act related to instinctual behavior? Did this gorilla react to the basic norms of society with respect to social values and ethics, or did it just do something that it would have done for any other young gorilla whose life may have been in jeopardy? When this gorilla was heralded as a heroine, BintiJua did not make any speeches acknowledging her appreciation for any reward. She did not say, "I saw my duty and I did it."

On the contrary, she accepted her reward in quiet grace and puzzlement, happy to receive whatever she got for doing something a human would consider a grand deed.

There was no great emotion involved in the gorilla's act. Although we can't deny that animals show signs of emotion, it is not the same as human beings. The dog wags its tail upon seeing its master; the cat purrs and rubs the leg of its master when it needs to be affectionate. There is no doubt that animals can think. If your cat or dog isn't fed they will try to stimulate your actions to feed them. Cats often meow until they hear the electric can opener opening their can of food. The same is true of humans: if we are hungry we will resort to finding ways for getting food. All living beings live by some aspect of the instinct to survive, but what causes this behavior?

Man wonders about the world he lives in: he has investigated the seas, oceans, and rivers; he has looked into the universe and answered questions concerning the cosmos. He has gone into the deep thicket of the jungle and found new and exciting phenomenons. He wonders about the planets, the sun, and the stars. Animals, however, are content to just survive. Why is this?

Man needs to love, to be loved, and to express love or hatred. Mankind deals with every facet of emotion, but do animals exhibit these emotions? If you have a pet I doubt that it has ever professed its love to you. You say perhaps it expresses its emotion through its behavior. It may lick your face, or nestle close to your body and give you the feeling of being in love with you, its master. But ask yourself this question: are animals capable of showing these feelings toward other animals? If the predatory beast were to consider the virtues of love it would perhaps go hungry. The animals in the wild do not consider which of them is strongest and therefore should have dominance; it is with brutal force and natural instinct that animals determine their territory and control. Why do human beings think logically and rationally and with specific purpose or will, while animals do not?

To understand the answer to the question, one must deal with the fact that there are two different types of spirits. Humans are incarnated with spirits that are a part of the Creator's spirit, while animals are incarnated with just a part of the living spirit of the Almighty. You might ask-what is the difference between the two? Listen to what the superior spirit Santorino has to say about spirits and their different perspectives:

Santorino

(July 4, 1954)

"One cannot create something out of nothing. The Almighty had at His disposal only the formless, lifeless, immobile matter, and His living spirit, and nothing else. There was absolutely nothing else in the world, if altogether it could have been called a world. Can you imagine the Almighty's dreadful, unbearable situation and loneliness in this lifeless, endless and formless, empty world? He was alone, completely alone, without any friends, without enemies. His living spirit could not endure that, and He smashed the silence and immobility. He perturbed the matter and, having given it the so-called laws of physics, made it form and able to move. Yet, no matter what form the matter assumed, it remained the very same matter. This matter had to be spiritualized with the living, intelligent, immortal spirit. Not only did it have to be set in motion and subjected to certain laws, but it had to be transformed as well.

"In order not to be alone, The Almighty created spirits from His spirit, the so-called original spirits the chief spirits. As you have been told already, these chief spirits did not rescue the Almighty from loneliness, for they were the very same Almighty, split into several parts. The Almighty searched long to find the means of escaping from this tragic situation. Finally He found it: He decided to create spirits and to join these spirits, for a definite and different time, with beings created from matter and capable of life. In this manner the spirits came under the influence of matter and matter under the influence of spirit. Yet prior to all of that, the Almighty had to create the living matter, which you know as the plant and animal kingdom. In order not to repeat Himself everywhere and always, and not to make His labor of creation uninteresting and meaningless, He transformed matter into such a state that, under the influence of certain laws of physics, it could devel op further and transform by itself should you follow the development of plants and animals on your Earth, you will clearly see how this task occurs and succeeds. The lifeless matter is pure matter, but the living matter is no longer pure matter-it has the Almighty's spirit blended within certain proportions. That is not the same as it is with man. In his being too, The Almighty is blended, to some extent, yet in addition to that man has been given a soul, that is, an Almightys spirit created separately, which incarnates in man for a time. This spirit influences the material side of man's being, and obviously, is himself influenced by it as well. This spirit, though-this soul-is not born at the same time as is man, and does not die at the same time with him. Thus, this soul, this spirit, returns to Heaven, but he is no longer exactly the same spirit, for he has already acquired something foreign, something new." (Mezins 1992, pp. 141-142)

The body (matter) through instinct alone cannot develop or create. This is shown clearly in the animal kingdom. Animals have survived since creation, and they possess no ability to change their world, or at least their immediate environment. It is also shown that as man's body developed so did his cognition. Men as beasts developed into human beings, but dogs are still dogs. Here the reason is shown why man can design, create, and develop his world. The spirit is incarnated in the human body and with the combination of spirit and matter the human has the power to change, develop, and think, since his brain has been spiritualized by the Almighty to do just that. It is also the reason why mankind has always believed in some omniscient and omnipresent life form, even in his primitive state; otherwise, how did he become so cognizant of the fact that his religious beliefs were a misinterpretation of his ancestor's understanding? In other words, why did his religious convictions change as he and the world grew?

Jesus, Buddha, and Confucius did not contrive an influence over the people through political or military power, so why is it that what they taught has influenced the cognition of mankind? Was it because mankind was aware of their coming and therefore commanded to obey and believe their teachings? Did mankind just simply become dissatisfied with his previous beliefs and teachings, thereby giving way to men with new and radical viewpoints?

It is my opinion, after considerable contemplation of these Messages, that the spirit in man is attempting to carry out its responsibility and obligation; that is, to help create and lead the ideal world. Through the course of human development we have acquired knowledge about our world; moreover, man has learned to utilize his emotions to determine the directions by which this knowledge would be implemented, notions such as love, egotism, shame, hate, envy, and greed. Animal behavior is not dependent on these emotions to determine their behavior; they live by instinct alone.

The spirit in its pure state has no need for the previously mentioned emotions. The spirit has no material needs: it does not need food, a house, a car, nor clothing, so it does not behave as matter in its pure state. Matter in its pure state tries to overpower the spirit that is incarnated into it. It attempts to slow down the progress of the spirit. It wants not to move or be alive. It tries to repel the spirit of the Almighty that gave it life. The matter influences the spirit by trying to control the spirit through the emotions that strips the spirit of ascending to the level of divinity. Envy, greed, hatred, and egotism are some of the emotions that the body (matter) uses to destroy the living spirit of the Almighty. The spirit has tried to find way to conquer these instincts in matter so as to be in harmony with God's will and the Almighty's wish to help matter reach the level of understanding the spirit world. Here is what the superior spirit Santorino has to say about this subject:

Santorino

(June 8, 1944)

"Human beings consist of two substances - spirit and matter. He/she has to strive to combine these two substances into one that can be sovereign and Almighty. For the time being, most human beings are still at the beginning of this road and are slaves of matter. Only a few individuals have been able to combine a high spirit with advanced matter, and are pulling mankind forward and elevating it, not withstanding the heavy power of inertia.

"The spirit is creative and cannot stand quiet and standing in the same place. It is active and searching.

"Matter is inert. It likes inactivity, and once moved cannot stop; therefore it is contrary to everything that disturbs its inert position.

"The spirit has a hard fight with the inclination of matter, and therefore there are very few instances where the spirit rules over matter, but there are many instances where matter rules over the spirit; the way has just started, notwithstanding the passage of thousands of years.

"What distinctive signs would reveal the spirit and matter of a human being?

"Spiritual signs are the following: a good nature, mercy, love, disinterest in materialist gains, a feeling of justice, a continuous longing for knowledge and omni comprehension, a disposition to sacrifice, conscious faith in God-Creator and leader of all-and a feeling of immortality.

"The signs of matter are the following: egotism, greed, degradation or cruelty, laziness, lack of interest, worship of inactivity, sensuality, a rather blind and sedate faith in God, or atheism and no feeling of immortality, and also jealousy and its twin, envy.

"According to these signs you can easily gauge every human being and determine if he/she is ruled by spirit or matter, and in what proportion these substances are.

"These indications are not as important to understand for the purpose of judging someone else, as to understand oneself. They show what the human being has to work against in an unrelenting struggle." (Homics 1976, pp. 200-201) (Mezins 1992, pp.54-55)

This world as we have learned at one time consisted of three elements: the spirit of the Almighty, matter, and energy. Matter has existed since before the Almighty created spirits from His spirit, but matter did not exist in the same state as it does now. Matter had no purpose or function; it existed in an inert state. The Almighty created the law of inertia, thereby giving matter movement and mobility. In order for matter to move in the animal state, the Almighty created the brain, but the Almighty saw that all matter could do was eat, sleep, and protect itself. It could not change or develop itself or the world in which it lived. The Almighty then decided to give this matter a part of His creative spirit, so that the two elements combined would grow to cooperate as a whole and help build the ideal world. This is why the human being have ruled and changed his world: the spirit that resides in the body, this wonderful creation of the Almighty is leading matter (our bodies) to a co-existence with the spiritual world.

Once again the insights of man are correct yet inaccurate. What we have come to understand in relation to man's origin can now be better understood. The spirits of the Almighty have revealed to us the purpose, design, and creation of the spirit and body. It is now mankind's task to reach a level where this information can be comprehended and acknowledged by everyone who resides within the Almighty's created world. Jesus, the Son of God, taught us to care for one another, but he did not teach us that God would save mankind from our own devised fate and creation. What He taught His disciples and mankind was how we should live together in peace and brotherhood. Jesus did not teach us about the true origin of mankind because people of that time would not have understood the truth as it has been presented to you now.

** All matter is consisted of the same materials atoms, which are comprised of protons, neutrons, and electrons.

** The human body as well as animals and plants are consisted of the same materials, atoms, which creates molecules, and part of the Creator's spirit.

** Matter in its pure state is inert; it is immobile. In order for matter to move the Creator blended a portion of His spirit with matter and gave it life or movement.

** The Almighty created the laws of physics and gave purpose to this created matter.

** He created brains in the animal creature so that they could survive. Although animals had brains they still could not understand the nature of their creation.

** The animals could not come to understand this world alone. They could not investigate, search, explore, research, nor explain any aspect of this world.

** Matter is inert. Matter does not like to be disturbed, but once the Almighty combined His spirit with matter it had to move. It has tried to repel the spirit of the Almighty.

** The Creator decided to give the brain of the body a part of His creative spirit. With this brain the spirit can help the matter to understand the spirit world.

** Although humans and animals are made up of matter and a blend of the Almighty's spirit, human beings are also incarat ed with a part of the Creator's creative spirit.

** To gauge one's self with respect to being controlled by spirit or matter one must assess his behavior or emotions.

** Signs of the spirit are as follows: good natured, merciful, loving, disinterested in materialistic gains, a feel for justice, a continuous longing for knowledge and omni comprehension, a disposition to sacrifice, a conscious faith in God, and a feeling of immortality.

** Signs of matter are as follows: egotism, greed, degradation or cruelty, laziness, lack of interest, worship of inactivity, sensuality, a rather blind and sedate faith in God, or atheism and no feeling of immortality, and also jealousy and its twin, envy.

GOD AND SATAN

Our religious institutions teach us to do good deeds and to reject evil thoughts and actions, yet in our approach to overcome evil we are forced to adhere to standards that are contradictions to the principles of Jesus Christ's teachings. In the view of human life we make promises to God to transform ourselves, to obey His wishes, to do good deeds, yet we are constantly doing deeds that are not within the keeping of His wishes.

Hunger, poverty, destitution, and injustice have become an acceptable norm within our human society. We often allude to the fact that God will help us to overcome these problems within society when He returns to us. I have questioned, however, my knowledge about this matter. If, for example, we are commanded by God to "do unto others what we ourselves would have done to us," why are we not doing as such? It is a simple command and, if we obey this command, then are we not doing the good for others and ourselves? Is Satan such an influence in man's life that we must wait on God to triumphantly defeat Him for us? Is evil then an attribute of mankind that can only be eliminated with God's direct intervention? Are we as human beings left with the decision to do good only if we can prove that it is within the keeping of our own thoughts and perceptions? In other words, are we supposed to do good by asking God to help us do as He commanded?

Doing good relates to deeds that will provide for the happiness of all humankind. Doing good does not simply mean that we must pray to and worship God. It does not mean that one can go to church each Sabbath day and confess one's sins in order to receive redemption and salvation. It does not mean that by learning the scriptures and verses of the Bible it will convey to God a sign of our doing good. Doing good is an active and conscious thought about the deeds that demonstrate our ability to overcome suffering for the whole human race. In doing good we help God to bring our fellow human being to a higher level of faith in goodness, eternity, and love.

We worry about the ensuing threat of poverty and ruin. We are attempting to gauge the world's economies in order to stay abreast of our investments. Jesus told His disciples that one day mankind would be able to perform miracles thousands of times greater than what He performed for the sick, impoverish, and suffering people. Man has now reached a stage where it can provide food for tens of thousands at a single event, whereas Jesus fed only five thousand who came to hear Him speak, and charged them nothing. Humanity has the power to cure many of the illnesses, which Christ performed as miracles, for no payment of any kind, yet mankind allows people to suffer if they are not insured or capable of paying for medical care. Thousand of people starve everyday even in the so-called developed nation while food is being made a stock commodity in the stock market throughout the world only for profit.

Evil, then, is man's inability or unwillingness to do those deeds which support God's wishes. When we allow people to suffer at the expense of our own desires, then we are doing evil deeds. It is not God's wish or will that any person suffers

-he did not create for humankind one society for the rich and one for the poor. These conditions were conceived through man's own concept and desires. It has come time for man to recognize that he is the perpetrator of this evil that resides within his created world. Does man ask for divine miracles to save himself? Are miracles needed to help us decide our fate? There need not be miracles to do good or eliminate doubt about the concept of doing good-waiting for miracles only slows down the progress of mankind.

Consider this point if you will: if your children are learning to do a task, do you make it easy for them, or do you make the task challenging enough so that the child can learn from their mistakes? If the task assigned them is difficult and somewhat of a struggle would you complete the task for them, or would you offer some slight assistance in helping them accomplish the ordeal of learning to be competent, successful, and independent? Let's take a toddler for example: a toddler must learn the social graces of using a knife and a fork to eat. You as a parent have the responsibility of teaching this child how to utilize eating utensils. You cannot teach her effectively by feeding her yourself. No, you must provide the resources, tools, and the proper motivation for this child to learn how to feed herself. Once you have done this, then you must provide the instructions on how she must accomplish this feat. Having always been fed by you, she now has to acquire the skills necessary to do it herself. Out of frustration, the initial attempts are met with anger and stubbornness. Your child wants desperately for you to intervene and give to her the comforts of not having to do this thing herself. If you intervene and help your demanding child, don't you think that would be to her disadvantage? How would she ever learn if every time she needed help you stepped in and provided her the sweet elation of your miracle? By constantly helping her to do something that she is capable of doing, only minimize, her efforts, thereby making the task more difficult. The same applies to mankind: God cannot and will not provide miracles to help us achieve our goal of overcoming evil.

One has to move in the direction of Gods will to overcome the forces of evil. Evil is not only the sins of doing those things which are deemed unlawful and not in accordance to God's com mandments, but also the actions through which man does not conform to the principles of bringing happiness to the whole of humankind. Evil is selfishness, greed, oppression, deprivation, hate, and a lack of faith in God's love and His will to eliminate suffering and unhappiness for all of humanity.

Now is the time for people to realize that God is not coming to save us, and that we must accept our own fate and destiny, for we have the free will to grow in happiness or fall into decay. It is within our power to save ourselves. We will either become helpers to God or we will fall into the abyss of non-existence. The time has come for mankind to see the real faces of God and Satan. God has once again revealed to mankind His true identity. This time we shall learn who God and Satan are, what They do, where They are, and why They exist.

The high spirit Santorino, who acts on behalf of God, reveals the following message to mankind:

Santorino

(May 29, 1944)

"I, Santorino, am speaking to you on behalf of God—the Messengers of the Almighty to the nations of the Earth. Permission has been given for human beings to look upon the face of God; listen and let everybody know when the time comes to speak.

Never should a human being struggle to understand the Almighty. That will be in vain, because human beings are not allowed to understand the Almighty. He is neither visible nor understood. The only sign of His existence is His living cross on the top of the Temple Deoss that might be felt and might be seen. That cross changes its brightness and color all the time, in that way sending signals to the spirits about the level of His thoughts. Three times the cross has faded and the world and the entire universe became still with a feeling of death, but the anger of the Almighty vanished at the last moment and the world could breathe again, speaking in the language of the humans. The cross is encircled by the sphere of an invisible element. Every spirit who wants to approach the cross is stricken by this unbelievably hard but invisible wall and smashed into dust.

The Temple of Deoss is in the center of the endless universe and it is far away from the closet stars. It is very beautiful-it glitters like the most beautiful jewel, and is so immense that your galaxy would fit into it easily. It is real and at the same time unreal, because it is built of rays that are inexpressible beautiful and lustrous. Its stairs remind one of a carpet woven by a rainbow. At the back wall there are two thrones: to the right is the throne of God and to the left is the throne of Satan. Behind the throne of God there is a bright, white shimmering background. Behind the throne of Satan the background is fiery red. Between them there is the scale of fate on which the rays of the superior spiritAlfa balance.

There are two rays: one is white, the other is red. Under the weight of these rays, the balance of the scale constantly tips one way or the other. Alfa never leaves His temple, and the same for the Almighty-nobody has seen Him and nobody understand Him.

God and Satan are shaped like human beings. They look very stately, beautiful and young, without beards or moustaches. Their bodies are five times taller than the diameter of your sun and they can be seen from the most distant corners of the temple.

The face of God is as light as the sun, and His smile soothes sorrow and pain as a mothers hand caresses a sick child.

The face of Satan is dark and as hard as a rock, From His eyes, rays of death and ice are streaming. Your scientists call these rays cosmic rays.

High above and between these thrones is the throne of the superior spirit

Omega, on a blue background. He Himself is not seen on the throne; only

His black shadow is there, and from there His voice sounds forth.

Streams of spirits enter and leave the Temple of Deoss without interruption. Around the Temple itself there is a complete emptiness and nobody is seen coming or going. This seems strange to you and hard to understand, but it is very easily explained. The spirit moves with the speed of thought; i.e., in a moment he is there where he wants to be. Along the way nobody sees him and he sees nobody. At the Temple of Deoss the spirits issue forth from endlessness as snowflakes from a cloud, where not a single snowflake can be found.

My throne is at the stairs of the throne of God. Around me the high envoys of God gather, among them Zarathustra, Buddha, Confucius, Mohammed, and the others. You will look in vain for Christ, because He was the son of God and has returned to His father." (Homics 1976, pp. 172 - 173) (Mezins 1992, pp.43-44)

Here again you must understand that the spirit world is immaterial; therefore, what has been revealed and described is only in the sense of human conception. How does one describe the color blue to someone who has been blind all of their life? What the superior spirit Santorino has done is give a description of the spirit world in terms of human understanding as how a spirit sees is different than how a human sees. As you explore more of this information you will come to understand the relationship between spirit and man and how they differ. At this point, however, it is important to note that there is a difference in perspective as it relates to physical and spiritual entity. The spirits have to convey to us in our sense and proportion of comprehension. In many cases they must resort to explaining situations and circumstances in terms of human perceptions. Although much of what is said can be viewed from a human perspective, it is done with the intention of elevating the human to an understanding of the spirit world.

The chief spirits Alpha and Omega have revealed to us how the Almighty came to create this universe. What we must come to realize is God and Satan's existence relates to specific functions and duties. In order to comprehend God and Satan, first we must understand their relationship to the Almighty. God and Satan (as well as all spirits) have been created from the spirit of the Almighty.

This then tells us that God did not create the universe, although God has been responsible for the lives of all living things on the Earth, in the sense that He is responsible for their creation and development. It has been through God that the earth exists, He has been responsible for creating life on our planet. It does not, however, mean that He created all of the galaxies, and solar systems in the universe. The spirit of God however, is the same as the spirit of the Almighty. He is that part of the Almighty, which provides all living beings with love within our galaxy. He is the one who helps us to understand His law of love. In fact, He is the Almighty and at the same time not the Almighty.

However paradoxical this may sound, we as mankind must now comprehend this concept. In coming to accept this truth we will realize the true function of God and Satan.

Listen to what the high spirit Volturnato has to say about the duties and responsibilities of God and Satan. Volturnato, however, is a superior spirit of

Satan. Since you will learn that God and Satan have different duties you must also come to understand that God and Satan have spirits that are designated to work with them.

Volturnato

(September 2, 1944)

"I, Volturnato, on behalf of the high ruler of heaven, Satan, am speaking to you, the Messengers of the Almighty to the nations of the Earth! Good and evil are completely relative ideas. In this world there is no absolute good and no absolute evil. What might be good to one might be evil to another.

"The function of God and His spirits are: to protect living things from perishing; to save them and help them to bring the idea of love and mercy to human beings; to make life pleasant, beautiful, and bright; to alleviate pain; to overcome doubt and inspire faith in goodness and in eternity; to present human beings and spirits to the Almighty and help them reach the gates of paradise.

"The function of Satan and His spirits are: to bolster living things; to form the strength of the body and the spirit; to destroy the inferior; to test the weak ones; to build up human beings and spirits through the mind and suffering; to punish the disobedient and harmful; to re-educate, in life and in the Planes of the Moon, the weak, the floundering and those wavering; to give human beings an understanding of logic and the laws; to help the spirits in the unrelenting fight with matter; to shape matter on its way to development in the understanding of the spirit and cooperation.

"The duty of Satan and His spirits is not to punish human beings for their sins. The human and the spirit are only punishing themselves by not following the laws of the Almighty, but not by the laws of Satan. The only punishment that is used by Satan is the thousand-year silence and the hell of darkness. This hell is without devils, without witches, without bonfires, without kettles and the likes. In these thousand years, the sinful spirit tortures himself by agonizing over his sins. It is not an easy hell-It is a horrible hell, more horrible than the old hell of devils created by human beings. But it is only for those who have committed dreadful crimes against the law given by the Almighty and human beings.

"The spirit cannot be released from the body either by God or Satan; it can only be asked of the Almighty to free the spirit from its body. The liberation is done only by the high spirit Mortifero through His spirits-only He alone and nobody else.

"Never say punishment of God, but rather punishment of Satan', for God never punishes anybody." (Homics 1976, pp 363364) (Mezins 1992, pp. 70-71)

Satan's messenger, Voltumato, reveals to mankind something entirely new: as a spirit of Satan, He calls upon mankind to realize that Satan works for the benefit of humanity. He summons mankind to act in accordance with God, to show mankind what must be done in order to establish for himself that which is good and that which must be changed in our knowledge of God and Satan for all of humanity. Satan is not what we have come to believe: the perpetrator of evil. He does not beseech spirits or humans to follow Him to the gates of hell.

The power of God is omnipotent and omniscient, but it must be recognized that His power works only when we work with Him. God cannot change man's destiny nor create it; the free will of spirits make it impossible. We must envision ourselves as the only creators of peace, good will, love, and justice for each and every human being. Let us now hear what the messenger of God has to say to humanity, as revealed by the superior spirit Santorino:

Santorino

(January 6, 1967)

"If God does not exist, then, neither does the Almighty exist. Some people will deny the Almighty as well. Perhaps they will even try to rise up against the Almighty, should they find out that He is not such as they want Him to be. Perhaps they will even get the spirits to join their side, and they too will rise up along with the people against the Almighty.

"Nothing, though, can threaten the Almighty, for no one knows Him personally, and no one knows where He is, while being everywhere. Only a momentary will of the Almighty is need- edfor all living beings, and all the spirits, to disappear from the universe in a second. And the next second in the universe there will be new spirits of the Almighty, and new living beings will be born on the planets.

"The Almighty does not threaten humanity. He merely tells it like it is and what may occur. The Almighty has created the universe the way He desires, and He asks all creation to carry out His will, and to adhere to the laws given by Him.

"He has entrusted the guidance of your galaxy to its God, your God. God gave laws to humanity as to how it must live in order to carry out the Almighty s will.

"You and all the people have to understand that you have no other alternative than to carry out the Almighty's will.

"His will was made known to you through Christ. The teachings of Christ remain the main one, and the only one for all humanity.

"You, Messengers, have not been called forth to alter it, but merely to supplement it, and to point out to humanity the errors which have been committed.

"Your other main task is to give humanity the explanation for its existence, the goals of its existence. Some will ask: what goals does man have? Why does he exist and what must be achieved?

"You also have to explain to man that he has two goals: one specifically as a man, and the other as his spirit after the death of man.

"Your task is extremely difficult for, just as the prophets and Christ, you will have to struggle against hostile people who receive with hostility everything that is new. You will have to struggle against overly smart people who will demand proof from you that the Messages have truly been given by the Almighty, rather than thought up by you, yourselves. Similarly, critics will strive to grasp at everything that appears doubtful to them.

"I, however, give you one reply: all these people who do not believe, who cannot believe, who do not want to believe in the truthfulness of the Messages-they are free to not believe. I summon only those to follow me who are capable of believing in the Messages. I do not need all the people; I only need the more capable ones! Thus say I, the Almighty. Having passed these words of the Almighty to you, I suspend my message until the next time." (Mezins 1992, pp. 365-367)

We can ill afford to relate our past and present religious experiences as being the will of God. God does not want us to continue to believe that He created Satan, nor that Satan resides in the core of the Earth. God cannot control Satan, nor can Satan control God. The two function in different ways. God possess all of the good of the Almighty and Satan possess all of the so-called evil of the Almighty.

The will of God calls for man to adhere to the laws of love. It is man who has taken out of context the true nature of God's will. We have done two things wrong in the process of carrying out the will of God: one, we have forgotten the lessons of Jesus Christ, and two: we have not completely adhered to the laws of God. They both relate to the same thing; however, they both must be considered separate acts. But something else must be reconciled: humanity is not to assume that all of mankind will face doom and destruction because we have not complied with God's will. Humanity is still on the road of discovering how to follow the law of God. God has the right to protect all living things and to help them understand the way to a beautiful life, while Satan has the right to test, punish, and destroy all those who do not wish to follow the laws of God. These Messages simply state what we must do to act in accordance with God's laws. We must eliminate selfishness. How? By not allowing it to exist. We must eliminate hate. How? By not allowing it to exist. We must eliminate destitution. How? By not allowing it to exist.

We may consider that the various entities of selfishness, greed, and destitution are established institutions within society. We must, however, consider ways to banish them. They certainly will not be toppled instantaneously - it would be ludicrous to assume that these institutional walls will fall like the walls of Jericho. But these Messages show what must be eliminated in the process of becoming compliant with God's will. In the millions of years it has taken mankind to reach this level of comprehension, it can be seen that we still are very far from reaching the ideal of He that created us. On the other hand, we still must venture beyond our current understanding. We must take to heart this information in order to become enlightened about our specific purpose and functions as human beings. We are not required to suffer unless we choose to. Humanity has a base for the so-called rich and a base for the socalled poor. This disparity has come as a result of two factors alone-greed and selfishness. Why? I ask you to put two like animals in a cage-it doesn't matter what kind or species. Now give them both only enough food for just one. You will see that the basic instinct for each is to control the other. One will dominate the other and eat all of the food while the other one will whither away and die or be killed. Mankind at times is ruled by his primitive instinct. Using only his primitive instinct he feels that he must conquer and have more than others so that his basic life needs are met. Rather than recognize that he is capable of producing enough material to provide for everyone's basic needs, mankind does not equate the fact that he is simply the caretaker of this planet. Humanity is a co-worker of God; mankind assists the Almighty and God in helping to create the ideal world. Some of the people in history thought that they could possess and control the planet. Caesar, Constantine the Great, Hanibal, Napoleon the I, Hitler, and others thought that they could conquer the world. Fortunately, it is not mankind's fault for thinking this way, because for so very long we have not understood our relationship with the spirits and the universe. While God and Satan have been influential in our lives, both have done so with different objectives and goals.

    Satan has tested the will of mankind through the influence of matter. He has had to help build the body by allowing our material side to be tempted with earthly gains or material possessions. While He is tempting individual humans, He is also testing humanity. This test is being done to see if mankind is capable of following the laws of God. Since God's function is to help, save, and protect living things, He is unable to assess a human being as useless or hopeless; therefore, He, does not do what Satan does, and that is to test, punish, and destroy all spirit that are not able to comply with the Almighty's or God's will.

For centuries we have only recognized our bodies as the essence of life. We have not completely understood the longevity or the origin of our spiritual entities. Matter or body is temporary, while our spirit is eternal. But, from the time we were created, we have been on the road of discovering that we are comprised of two separate substances: spirit and matter. God and Satan's responsibilities have been to bring up these two substances to a point where they would reach a state of cooperation. For millions of years, however, we have done as our ancestors, and that is to ensure the survival of one's self. Satan in His role has allowed man to progress in this fashion in order to see if man would ultimately come to obey the rules of God; God, on the other hand, has been helping mankind to realize that doing good helps to ensure the longevity of all humanity. The influence of Satan has impacted our ancestors and what they have institutionalized can be and must be eliminated. God has helped mankind to recognize their mistakes and, in doing so, He guides us through these errors so that we can bring an end to the harm and suffering that human beings face on this planet.

God has at last revealed to mankind who and what He really is. This story is not complete by any stretch of the imagination; however, we can choose to go forward or stay situated in our present-day beliefs. Miracles are not needed to prove these passages because the miracles are around us every day. These miracles can be traced to the origin of their discoverer or inventor. Here we are, the adults of our ancestors, standing on a new road proceeding toward goodness and eternity. Our ancestors fought with the instinct of matter, and our ancestors were ourselves. We have grown up and now the perspective of life glistens before us. No longer shall we see darkness and lost voids in our paths but the brightness of God's love will illuminate the path into eternity.

God has again revealed to humanity the road toward love, peace, and happiness. Our comprehension of the Messages will provide for us the opportunity to rise above the turmoil, confusion, and grief that we are experiencing within our society. This light of truth can be like a shield against the battering ram of injustice, selfishness, greed, and hatred. The eternity of mankind is the kingdom, which resides within us. Our heaven or hell resides within our ability to recognize the truth, and to use the truth to create the ideal world as the Almighty has willed.

Now we must revise ourselves in thought, perception, and conception. God and Satan function to help us grow in spirit and matter. So, in order to do this, we are shown and enlightened by God and Satan so that we can recognize what it is we must do. We are given this opportunity to understand our purpose for existing on this planet and in the universe. The Messages have been revealed in order that mankind may move from the darkness of his own interpretation of life into the light of God's truth.

Let us then go forth and learn more of ourselves. We must proceed to the level of our spirits so that we may come to terms with our spirit life. In knowing and understanding Gods laws we must know ourselves. The creative spirit of the Almighty resides in man; the individual spirit of you resides in you. The will of the spirit must be free to grow, develop, and live eternally.

** God and Satan spirits were created from the spirit of the Almighty.

** God cannot rule over Satan, nor can Satan rule over God.

** Good and evil are relative-there is no absolute evil nor absolute good.

** God and Satan reside in a place known as the Temple of Deoss. This place is located far from the closet stars in the uni verse, situated in the middle of the endless universe.

** God and Satan have different duties and functions. God has all the good of the Almighty and Satan has all of the so-called evil of the Almighty.

** The functions of God are: to protect living things from perishing; to save them and help them, to bring the idea of love and mercy to human beings; to make their life pleasant, beautiful, and bright; to alleviate pain; to overcome doubt and inspire faith in goodness and in eternity; to present human beings and spirits to the Almighty and help them to reach the gates of Paradise.

** The functions of Satan and His spirits are: to bolster living things; to form the strength of the body and the spirit; to destroy the inferior; to test the weak ones; to build up the human being and spirits through the mind and suffering; to punish the disobedient and harmful; to reeducate in life and in the Planes of the Moon, the weak, the floundering and those wavering; to give to human beings an understanding of logic and the laws; to help the spirits in the unrelenting fight with matter; to shape matter on its way to development in the understanding of the spirit and the cooperation between matter and spirit.

It's a Matter of Life Before Birth

(Reincarnation)

Have you ever thought of the possibility that there is life before life? Many people through the ages have questioned the possibility of life after death, but never of life before birth. I know of only one person who had some connection with the possibility of life before birth. Mr. Edgar Cayce, who died in 1945, recorded some accounts of his efforts to recall the lives of people in their spiritual past. He provided case studies dealing with his ability to read the past histories of people's past lives, but was not able to prove or disprove his abilities. But suppose we were to think in terms of having an existence before we were born. We have explored the prominent thought of life after death to a point of scientific examination and experimentation. "As scientists study the meaning of near-death experiences, perhaps we can inch closer to an understanding of life," stated Verlyn Klinkenborg, in her article entitled "At the Edge of Eternity." Ms. Klinkenborg cites instances of continual growth in the area of studying what happens after death, or neardeath experiences. She states: "Where there was once only a few researchers working on the subject, there are now dozens worldwide: physicians, psychologists, sociologists, anthropologists, biologists, philosophers, theologians, parapsychologists, mediums, shamans, yogis, lamas, and not a few journalists.', (Time, Feb. 1992)

To understand death one must come to comprehend and acknowledge that one's individual spirit resides within one's body and that one's spirit may have resided in many other bodies as well. There is really no death; just the transference of the spirit from one body to another. We call this process reincarnation. How can reincarnation be proven? Empirical data to support this claim will be needed by both the religious and scientific community to gain their confidence and belief. Unfortunately, the spirit is neither visible or touchable, nor is it composed of any element which would subject it to disclosure by the human being. Each individual must see that a new direction for mankind's survival is being given to him. All people must begin to assess, evaluate, and conclude their ideas on what the Messages have revealed. The comprehension and acknowledgement of living eternally in spirit and body must be seen as the new objective and goal of humanity. We were told in the chapter dealing with the creation of the universe and spirits about the aim and sense of human life. The chief spirits Alpha and Omega stated that, "Man's task is, by combining the spirit and matter, the body to rise above the existing laws of nature and to create an ideally perfect and eternal being. To create a being who will ascend to the level of divinity and jointly with the Almighty will undertake the further formation and ruling of the universe. Such is the goal and sense of human life. For the time being, while it still has not been possible to overcome matter and to form an immortal body, the spirits have to travel from one body to the next." (Homics 1976, pp. 50-5 1) (Mezins 1992, pp. 192)

For centuries the subject of reincarnation has caused considerable consternation within the framework of society's beliefs and knowledge. For the most part, much of mankind has been taught to believe only in the Holy Spirit of God, Jesus Christ, and other envoys. We are told that the Holy Ghost will dwell within us, and by being saved or becoming Christians we will ultimately get to live with God for all eternity after He returns to earth. Our spiritual entity is not fully recognized, and we are told that the spirit of God will dwell within our hearts if we follow His rules, and then we will earn the reward of living eternally after He returns to save those that have followed His law of love. Now is the time for mankind to learn of their immortal spirit, and the fact that the laws of God are to be obeyed in order to obtain eternal individuality of one's spirit. This new religion requires all people to have faith in knowing that they will never die; also, everyone must comprehend that they have lived for generations already as living spirits or they are new spirits.

We are given to think that life comes as a moment of time. "We have but one life to live" is the common phrase used to establish the existence of our lives. We pour into this one life the very essence of ourselves to achieve the eternal gates of heaven or hell. Knowing not whence we came or when we are going, we touch on the possibility of insanity in our lust to know what we are, where we are from, and where we will end up.

By coming to believe in the Messages to Mankind From the Almighty and His Spirits, I was able to redefine my thinking into a logical conclusion about life and death. What has been revealed is not unlike our current day assumption pertaining to such matters. It is much more conclusive, however, because the revelations are coming from spirits themselves.

The Almighty has allowed His superior spirits to talk with mankind to let us know who we are, why we are here, and where we are going. It is in this vein that I am able to give to you my thoughts and beliefs as to these seemingly insurmountable questions about life before birth and life after death.

The message is simple: we are spirits residing in human bodies temporarily. Death is but the demise of the human body, not the destruction of the entire person. In recent years, people have studied the phenomenon of life after death. Raymond A. Moody Jr. approached the subject in his book entitled "Life after Life." In speaking of death, he states: "If we are to talk of death at all, then we must avoid both social taboos and the deep-seated linguistic dilemmas, which derive from our own experiences. What we often end up doing is talking in euphemistic analogies." He goes on to state, "Perhaps the most common analogy of this type is the comparison between death and sleeping. Dying, we tell ourselves, is like going to sleep. This figure of speech occurs very commonly in everyday thought and language, as well as in the literature of many cultures and many ages." (Moody 1975, pp. 16)

Even though mankind has put forth an effort to explain the phenomenon of spirits, we are still left with a void instead of an adequate answer. As Dr. Moody notes, "This persistent aspect has been called by many names, among them psyche, soul, mind, spirit, self, being, and consciousness. By whatever name it is called, the notion that one passes into another realm of existence upon physical death is among the most venerable of human beliefs." (Moody 1975, p.17)

Our religious institutions have little or no conviction in the understanding of spirits and reincarnation. They have assumed that with death comes the inevitable salvation or destruction of the soul. The clergy cannot be faulted for their assumption, however, for they can believe only what has been revealed and taught to them. Scientists believe that through thought the brain is the controlling mechanism for the entire body, and its subsequent actions. Can we, however, afford to keep on believing either of these institutions with regard to the life forces that keeps mankind alive? They claim to know the answers to these questions and yet mankind is still mystified and confused about them.

Currently, we are at a point of indistinctiveness, groping for an understanding of life after death. Our spirits are the manifestation of the spirit that created all life in the universe. Therefore, mankind must recognize the immortality of its own spirit. We, as a part of the Almighty's spirit, have a duty to become cognizant of His desire to want us to live eternally with Him.

Meagerly we dismiss the possibility of eternal life, yet we pray for it every day of our lives. We raise the question of "What must I do to obtain eternal life?" In God's and Jesus Christ's spirits we live, but we do not live in the knowledge of our own immortality. Our spirits will see God upon our body's demise and yet we wait until the supposed apocalypse and the second coming of God to see our spirits and bodies rise from the grave and go with Him

Today's religious institutions acknowledge spiritual life after death but do not regard the possibility of spiritual life before birth. The clergy is understandably limited in their knowledge about such matters. They preach about the second coming of God, which will, in their understanding, bring about eternal life for those who have been faithful in following His commandments. Mankind has talked about atomic destruction and devastation, and then prayed for God to intervene and save our created civilization. Will God reappear and command a halt to the destruction of His creation? Man seeks to destroy man under the banner of "In God We Trust." They say that in life human beings are expendable, for they fight to ensure peace, freedom, and justice. They are, therefore, carrying out the will of God. But where is it written that God commands the creation of atomic or ultimate weapons to defend the rights of others? If it is written, then it is a blatant lie.

God's spirit, and all spirits are created from the same source. Therefore, our spirits are eternal, everlasting, and identical to the spirit of God. The body is only temporary, and until we can create immortal bodies we must continue the process of reincarnating into other bodies. Consequently, we must come to terms with a new realization about ourselves. Life is not short but as long as eternity itself. We need not pray for the intervention of God, but must begin to replace old ideas about life with this new revelation.

Will mankind once again allow the opportunity to rise above the earth, sun, and stars to deteriorate while seeking a beginning to a frightful end? Man does not live in body alone, nor is his conscience an entity within itself. The conscience of man is his living spirit that resides within the body, and yet is a separate entity from his body. The body may cease to exist but the spirit continues to live eternally. All spirits are created by the sanctity of the Almighty. Let us proceed forward on our new journey toward understanding the spirits and reincarnation, as revealed by the superiors and high spirits of the Almighty.

HIGH SPIRIT ALI

(February 27, 1944)

"Some scientists deny the existence of spirits and say that matter alone is forming man's physical and spiritual development. With this approach they make the problem more complicated, instead of simplifying it.

"Scientists understand the brain and the nature of its function. Though the atoms that form the brain are blind and deaf, what forces those brain atoms to think so logically and wonderfully?

"It is as if somehow the atoms condensate and change themselves, thus creating higher forms. It is the same understanding as for a being from an underdeveloped society upon seeing an electrical station for the very first time, would say that the smallest machine changes into a bigger one, and so these machines continue to create themselves and, therefore, are sensibly guiding their actions. The person, not knowing that upstairs is an engineer who created and is guiding these machines, would be understandable in their foolishness.

"What moves mankind to study the skies, the north pole, the depths of the oceans? -Studies that give nothing back for material well being? And what separates humankind from animals? What else allows humankind such unlimited development if not the spirit of God?

"Animals, with all their wits and development, have not achieved more than the most necessary requirements for life and struggle. The dog is the same as it was in the era of the caveman. The elephant, the wisest of animals, can collect logs to build a house, but cannot build even the simplest hut, because it does not have what humankind has -the spirit of the Almighty." (Homics 1976, pp. 49-50) (Mezins 1992, pp. 20-21)

What the high spirit Ali reveals is something that has been discussed previously. He gives, however, a better explanation of what has to be considered with regard to spiritual and matter's co-existence: matter alone cannot transform itself nor can the spirit develop and grow without the help of matter, as the two substances share a mutual and dual function. If we learn to cooperate and progress together then we will be in keeping with the Almighty's will. Just think of what this idea implies: we can begin to think in terms of immortality not as a fantasy or abstract idea but as a reality. Our spirits are immortal; therefore, we are already eternal beings, which leaves us to discover how to create immortal bodies for the spirit.

Picture this: your body and spirit in the future will have complete cooperation. Your spirit will be able to be independent of its body, thereby, allowing your spirit to experience both essences of life-that is, spiritual life and material life. One million years from today you will be able to look back on the developmental years of turmoil and frustration and giggle at how primitive we were. Instead of living on one planet we will be living on many planets within our galaxy. We will traverse the solar systems within our galaxy, with our spirits and bodies working together. One part (spirit) will view hostile planets with their noxious gases and intolerable surfaces, and upon reentering the immortal body, it will contemplate the resources available and deduce ways to make it beneficial for humanity. Matter can only transform matter with the help of the spirit, and vice versa.

The spirit grows and progresses with the help of matter. The two combined makes it possible for the human to use his will, mind, and intellect to create the ideal world. The ideal world pertains to mankind's ability to change the natural laws, which are unfavorable to him, in order to achieve ideal happiness for humanity. The ideal world pertains not only to the earth but also to the entire universe. By coming to terms with these ideas, we begin the course toward understanding and cooperating with the spirit. Our spirit uses the brain to work and transform matter; matter uses the spirit to understand the world of matter, therefore freeing itself of material desire and interest. The only need that matter has is to understand how to achieve immortality. No matter what happens, the physical will always experience the physical. The spirit cannot, based on its composition, experience the physical nature of matter; consequently, the spirit will need matter (bodies) to experience the pleasures of matter. The poets will continue to write their poems, the musicians will always write the appropriate songs for the heart, and men will always love beautiful women. With the cooperation of spirit and matter we can experience the world entirely differently. There can be no set bounds for the creative spirit of the Almighty. That creative spirit which resides in mankind must be understood and recognized.

Mankind has been instructed in what spirits are consisted of and how we as spirits function. The Messages show to us a portion of what it is we will be able to do once we become spirits again. The Almighty's superior spirit Santorino illuminates this aspect of the Messages:

Santorino

(February 19, 1944)

"Now I will lead you into the spirit world. Follow me carefully. I will speak to you as if you were my students. Let's start.

"The spirits are not the kind you are thinking about. They are not angels with wings, nor are they devils with tails. The spirits are invisible because they have no bodies. They look like people on Earth; that is, we see each other that way. The spirits do not think as people because they have no brains-they have only comprehension and omniscience. In order to grow, to think, and to change, the spirit has to be reincarnated. The spirit moves with the speed of thought. He can be here and someplace else, if he wants to, at the same time. Super-spirits are omnipresent.

"It seems strange to you, but take your teaching of today. What do you know of the atom? In Greek it means indivisible. But you know now that the atom is a microscopic system of the sun. It is created by electricity. Rocks and steam are the same atoms. Hard steel and impermeable air are the same entity of electricity.

"How can the spirits move so fast and speak from endless distances? Take your telephone. With the help of electricity you can speak with a man who is a thousand miles away from you. He answers you as if he was sitting across the desk. Can you imagine that?

"You are sleeping and your eyes are closed, but you see people and talk to them. You see things and places in your life that you have never seen before. When you wake up, you feel that the dream was the same as real life. With what did you see the other world? Of course, not with your eyes. But seeing, hearing, and speaking by the spirits are difficult to explain to you. This knowledge is not necessary for you to know.

"How do spirits speak with a human being? Usually with anticipation. The Almighty announces His will through His envoys, such as Christ and others, who speak specially in His name, or else through spirits, who, having incarnated in humans reveal the Almightys will, and geniuses. Or else, as in your case, through you with the saucer [and the circle of letters.]" (Homics 1976, p. 40) (Mezins 1992, pp. 12-13)

Santorino

(February 20, 1944)

"The spirit consists of two elements: the spirit of the Almighty, which is not understandable to anybody, and the electric atom. From them the spirit builds the needed body for him/herself. That happens instantaneously. The spirit is able to condense the atoms so that it can become visible even to human beings. A human being cannot control the atoms of his/her body, but a spirit is able to rule over them completely.

"The soul, or the spirit of the Almighty, exists unchanged by itself, or as a soul of a living human being.

"In the form of Himself, God or Satan is everywhere and speaks to everyone. Like the voice on a radio station, it is carried to every house where there is a receiver. In the same way the voice of God is heard by everyone who has a heart to pick it up.

"You see, electricity forms the matter, makes the light, creates the heat, drives the motor' gives wings to humankind, carries voices across the oceans, and does and forms many other things about which you have no knowledge.... After the death of a human being, the first-time-born spirits are as weak as a human being. After being in the Planes of the

Moon they have grown, and they continue for thousands of years until all the Planes are completed. Then the Sun Planes start the life of the spirits as spirits of living beings. As for those who do not stay in the Sun Planes forever, they start to serve the Almighty as spirits, and the final aim is paradise." (Homics 1976, p. 42) (Mezins 1992, pp. 14-15)

Our imagination has led us to believe, speculate, and suppose many ideas with respects to how we came to exist. The answers to the question of life and death seemed to be monumental until now. Human beings can now put aside all of the philosophical, scientific, and religious phenomenon and discussion and begin focusing on the practical approach revealed to us by the Almighty's superior spirits.

At last we can claim for humanity the idea of immortality; immortality based on truth gives us the tools for creating an ideal world for humanity. We no longer have to search for a conclusion on how life begins and ends.

For thousands of years we have wondered and guessed at answers to our existence. Scientists and the clergy have given us a sense of knowledge as it relates to our human experiences and encounters, but now we must recognize that the very essence of our lives relate to our Creator revealing to us that which was never known. Each of us can now begin to relate to how and why we exist. Our existence did not start on the day of our birth on this planet, inside our bodies. In the course of thousands of centuries we as human beings have made attempts to understand our spiritu al entity. Our spirits are trying to help matter reach the level of immortality, completing the process of understanding its spiritual entity. So in spiritual terms we are born not to die, but to live forever. Our duty as human beings is to come to comprehend this aspect of truth.

** One must come to understand that in actuality there is no death. Every living human being has residing in them a living spirit that is immortal.

** Each spirit is created from the same spirit that creates and has created all spirits.

** The human's task is to reach the level of the spirit, by corn bining the strength of spirit and matter, to compel the body to rise above the existing laws of nature and to create an ideally perfect and eternal being, a being that will reach the level of divinity and together with the Almighty take over the further formation and ruling of the universe.

** Matter and spirit share a mutual and dual function. The spirit helps the matter to change, and the matter helps the spirit to grow and develop.

** The spirit cannot, based on its composition, experience the physical nature of matter; consequently, the spirit needs matter (bodies) to experience the pleasures of matter.

** The spirit consists of two elements: the Almighty's spirit, which is unknown to anyone, and the electric atom. The soul or the Almighty's spirit is what exists invariably, either on its own or as the soul of a living being.

** The spirit and matter goes through centuries of transforma tion as it continues to be reincarnated in human bodies.

Memory Of The Spirit

If your spirit was created one hundred thousand years ago, would your brain be able to deal with the present and past events of your life? How would you fit into your human consciousness the knowledge of your extended past? It is better to read about it in scientific books, than to remember such an existence in your present life. Imagine the consequences of having such a memory: you would have to filter out all of the insignificant data of the past in order to concentrate on the present. If you had been incarnated in the primitive man then it might be impossible to relate to the present inventions and discoveries. You would have to deal with going to the grocery store instead of hunting for food. Tall buildings would replace the forest and the jungle of your past world. How could you relate to that? The spirit sees and knows all that is going on in the world. It does not need its new body to have knowledge relating to past experiences. Past experiences do not die-they just become idle or dormant in the spirit's omniscience, waiting to be reborn after the death of your body.

Perhaps the question that might come to your mind is: how is it that the spirit does not remember its past? Lets talk about why we are not able to relate our past spiritual experiences to present life. This question was put forth to the high spirit Ali:

ALI

(March 2b, 1944)

"How does it happen that the spirit, being reincarnated in the human body, forgets its past completely?

"In this way: too many engravings on the memory would disturb the human being. You attend a university. You store in your memory thousands of pages of knowledge. Now, during your life do you keep them in your brain and remember them only if you need them ? It is the same for your past on this planet. Your parents, childhood, teenage friends, sorrows, and pleasures are in your memory. In your daily life you do not remember days, months, or even years sometimes. They are dormant in your brain like corpses and, only during moments of meditation do they come alive again. What would happen if you would not be able to forget your past memories and were bothered every moment? Would you be able to live, and are these memories even necessary? The same happened with the memory of the spirit. It is switched off from the minute the spirit is reincarnated until the moment when the body starts to die. The spirits with a special duty may remember something." (Homics 1976, p. 74) (Mezins 1992, pp. 30-31)

There is no need to assume any more concerning the question of the spirits functions and capabilities: the Messages give to mankind explanations about such matters. Where once we were lost in a quagmire of possibilities, we can now find solutions to the puzzle that has so long eluded mankind. The Messages open up the possibilities of comprehending much that is needed to know about our spirits and our spiritual life. In the past as well as the present, we have considered the possibilities of spiritual life, but the future can become bright with a true knowledge of what our spirits are, its purpose, and function. There is nothing so vastly complicated about this information that would make it impossible for a literate person to comprehend. The explanation and reason for the spirit's existence is so simple yet complicated, and moreover, non-paradoxical.

** The memory of the spirit is switched off once it is incarnated in the body.

** Too much of the spirit's past from previous lives would only impede the function of the human's life.

** The memory of the spirit contains, in some cases, thousands of years' worth of information dealing with past lives in other bodies.

** The spiritual memory serves no purpose while one resides in the body. In comparison, what one does during one's life time is not remembered on a day-to-day basis. One has to forget much of one's life's activities in the course of one's daily life.

** In your daily life one forgets days, months, and even years of events. Memories of things such as friends, studies, and important events usually lie dormant within the mind until they are recalled for some specific reason.

Conclusion

For the past twenty-seven years, I have gained new knowledge and faith with respect to God, religion, mankind, spirituality, and creation. In coming to terms with these "Messages to Mankind from the Almighty and His Spirits" I have had to cast off my doubts and fears and choose to believe The Almighty's Religion for the Universe" (Supplementology). As I learned more about the questions that had so often plagued my mind about the convictions of my beliefs concerning standard and traditional faiths and religions, I have come to find new answers to the questions that have so perplexed mankind and me.

Aside from the influence of the Message Bearers and their children, I have come to understand and accept these Messages by myself. It has been with a sense of urgency that I have come to believe the Messages. Because of the ways and conditions of our world I had to explore new routes of understanding life. The meaning of our world, to me had little or no clarity as to the definitions of which I wanted to comprehend. Yes, I believed in love, respect, justice, and peace for all humanity, but there was very little being done concretely to illustrate for me that these basic notions and feelings were valid. As a human being, I considered all of the possible solutions to understanding my purpose for existing, and each endeavor put me on the pathway of discovering man's reasoning and understanding about life. Neither religion nor science provided me with a comfortable comprehension about life. My mind wandered from one possibility to the next; the circle of conventionality kept spinning me around. Relentlessly, I pursued the might of God within my mind to give me an answer to what I could do to instill peace and happiness within the framework of humanity. The Serenity Prayer stayed constantly within my conscience: "Dear God, help me to accept the things I cannot change, the courage to change the things that I can, and the wisdom to know the difference."

While I observed the deteriorating conditions of humanity I found no solace in knowing that God was returning to mankind to help him overcome the evil that had permeated the Earth. As a man I have come to know hatred, bigotry, greed, and poverty as the essence of life's elements. Science in all of its glory has not rid the inhabitants of this planet of their sorrows and worries.

Mighty mountains of concrete and steel blocked the vision of my universal desire. I was discontent with the way the world was progressing as I had a drive that exceeded all notions of living happily in a material world. As such, it has been to my good fortune to discover "The Almighty's Religion". I now reveal to mankind a discovery that we all have been searching for in our day-to-day lives. This religion gives to humanity a way by which we can all become brothers and sisters again. Despite our religious, ethnic, and cultural differences, we can come to comprehend our lives as being for one and the same purpose.

In the few words that this book contains, you may find a new direction for yourself, as well as for humanity. You will invariably feel that this information is incredulous. If you allow your mind and spirit, however, to investigate this information and compare it with our present day beliefs and understandings, it will show to you something new and wonderful.

Although I have discussed some aspects of the Messages, I did not include everything that has been revealed. You will discover as you proceed further that the Messages discuss every aspect of human civilization and social condition. Supplementology reveal how our churches, synagogues, mosques, and temples should operate; how all religions can unite and work cooperatively with one another; how to deal effectively with child rearing; the state of mankind's political system and what must be done to reform it; stories of the Message Bearers' past lives; and how mankind must formulate its social institutions. The Messages contain even more in that they show to what extent man has grown and developed and his potential for future progress. I would have revealed more on these subjects; however, I feel that each person must decide for himself or herself whether or not they will want to explore the entire content of the Messages for themselves. These Messages are not for everyone in that it will take some time to absorb and digest this information. The information is so radical that the only way to learn the Messages firsthand is to explore them on your own, and hopefully you will see that the challenge is not in the reading of this information but the acceptance and belief of it. Like everything new it will take some time to appreciate this information; however, as you begin to explore the Messages, you will come to adapt and adopt the information for the good of yourself and humanity.

I hope for the sake of humanity that you will at least take the time to study the Messages and assess Supplementology on the basis of what we as the human race can gain positively from it. Do not accept this religion on the condition of what I have come to accept. Do not accept this religion on the condition that there will be some type of reward or some kind of punishment for not accepting-instead accept it because it can provide you with a new insight about life. The Messages will allow you to think freely about those things, which you have perhaps considered possible. You will be able to use your imagination and conscience in unison. Your thoughts can reach beyond your immediate world. Although doubt may precede your faith in this new religious discovery, do not allow your mind to close off the possibilities of this new religion. Like everything new, it is considerably different and takes time to get use to. Do not, however, become frightened and disconcerted for this religion does not ask for an immediate change in your lifestyle-it just asks that you come to comprehend and acknowledge The Almighty's Religion for the Universe. (Supplementology)

We are being given this opportunity to understand the Messages on the basis of where we as "spirits" and human beings have developed. The Almighty, as we have been shown, does not need to frighten or reward anyone for believing or not believing the Messages. Our "spirits" are eternal and, as such, we have all eternity in which to comprehend the Almighty's Religion. On the other hand, if we do not come to understand the Messages, then we put the whole of humanity in certain peril. Peace, love, justice, and brotherhood can come about as a result of learning and obeying the law of love. This is the Almighty's law and He has placed the responsibility with our God to show us how to come to terms with it. If mankind continues, however, on the same path it is currently following then certain doom is inevitable. All humanity must come to recognize and comprehend this new direction given to man from the Almighty and His Spirits. In doing so, we will be in keeping with the Creator's desire to have us become helpers and assistants to Him through all eternity.

Maya Homics, Nick Mezins, and I have created the name for a new religion but we did not create this religion.

Their parents and others were responsible for receiving these Messages and now humankind is responsible for using them to bring about a change on this planet and throughout the universe. We are being observed and our actions and deeds will determine what The Almighty's decision will be as it pertains to the continued existence of this planet and it inhabitants. The name does not change what it is we have tried to provide to humanity. It is "The Almighty's Religion for the Universe."

I've Broken Through the Barrier

I've broken through the barrier
This barrier called time
To bring to life new recipes
Health food for the mind.
All the garbage and the dead things
that the mind has taken in
Will purge itself and purify
as these messages descend.
Through mind, soul, and Spirit
To life's regenerating force
Mind can now bring changes
to stop death at its source.
Awareness grows and humbles us
as infinity sinks in.
All spirits are connected
from where we all began
All souls link up together
like the air that we take in.
Minds all have their channels filled with
thought from where all
thoughts descend.
With unclean thoughts
our channels clog

interference stops our goal
Like meat that's putrefying
evil grudges fill our soul.
Death in real life and in pictures on TV
distorts our mental images
Not allowing us to see.
Through Death the Grand Illusion
Programmed from within
Master of this doorway
With each door new life begins.
Changing Face and Figure
Like we would adorn new clothes
each lifetime's but a whisper
As time travelers disrobe.
We gain appreciation
For each role that we play
in this grand initiation
As time sends us on our way.
Our faith and will do shape each life
As time itself consumes
and houses the Great Spirit
in infinity's grand room.

—B.A. Ware, February 1996

Acknowledgements

The contents of this book is intended for the general public. This book was written with the desire to reveal a new religious concept to all those that wish to follow a different course towards humanity's objectives for peace and goodwill. Therefore, I was unable to use, to any great extent, information relating to man's current authorities and religious faiths. I tried, however, to provide some illustrations relating to current discoveries about our planet and ourselves and as such, I have provided references of those materials I used. I am very grateful for the knowledge that this information provided to me. I would like to express my thanks and appreciation for their valuable assistance.

I must recognize the immensity of the task that the Message Bearers undertook. They were the first human beings to speak directly with other spirits of the Almighty. It is through their faith and conviction that these Messages are being presented to humanity. Therefore, I gratefully thank Mr. Alexander Upenieks, Mr. Alexander Homics, Mr. John Kuzis, Mr. and Mrs. John and Mary Mezins, Henry, Emily, and Nicholas for completing their courageous task.

I would like to also thank my wife, Olivia, my mother, and Perfect Love. Especially I thank all those that have provided their support and encouragement to me throughout these years.

References

Carrington, Richard. The Mammals. Time-Life Books (New York: 1963)

Ford, Adam. Spaceship Earth. Lothrop, Lee & Shephard (New York: 1981)

Homics, Alexander. Messages to Mankind from the Almighty and His Spirits. Vantage Press (New York: 1978)

Howell, F. Clark. Early Man. Time Life Books. (New York: 1965)

Klinenborg, Verlyn. At the Edge of Time. Time, Feb. 1992

Mezins, Nick. Revelations. Derek Publisher, Inc. (Nashville: 1992)

Moody, Raymond, Jr. Life after Life. Mockingbird Books, Inc. (Covington, Ga.)

Editors, Readers Digest, History of Man: The Last Two Million Years.

Readers Digest Association, Inc. (Pleasantville, N.Y.: 1973)

www.ingramcontent.com/pod-product-compliance
Lightning Source LLC
LaVergne TN
LVHW021715060526
838200LV00050B/2674